The Old Village Road

Songs of a Vietnamese American

Hao C. Tran

The Old Village Road, Copyright 2026
Autonomous Press, LLC (Fort Worth, TX, 76114).

Autonomous Press is independent and worker-owned.
No AI was used in the creation of any part of this book.

Paperback: 978-1-945955-58-7
Ebook: 978-1-945955-59-4

Cover drawing by an unknown Saigon street artist.
Interior by Casandra Johns

Contents

Foreword:
A Teacher's Soul

The first place I met Hao was at our Aikido dojo in 2017. I'd been practicing for many years when he showed up brand new (*in his sixties*—a fact that will become less surprising as you read on). So, ironically, our relationship began with me as his Sensei: something he still affectionately calls me sometimes, though it's since been proven many times over that the opposite is true.

In 2020, knowing that he liked to write, I invited Hao to be part of the experiment that became my first writing group. As with all the communities he's part of, he quickly became a foundational presence there, changing us weekly with his stunning words.

Most recently I've been learning Tai Chi from Hao.

"Breathe in," he'll say to the group, as we hold a ball of energy beside our rib cages. "Breathe out," he invites, as we extend our arms out to grasp the peacock's tail. *Breathe in*, as our cloud hands move to the right. *Breathe out*, as they rotate left.

Go slower, he's always reminding us. *Slower*.

Hao is someone who lives breath by breath. Who gives

himself fully to whatever is important to him, or whatever he finds beautiful. He picks it up quickly, undistractedly, and, with a patient dedication that is rare for our species, practices to the point of impeccability.

Having witnessed his writing over the years—including the book you are about to read—I think I'm beginning to see how he does this. It's not something I can hope to replicate, but to say it's been enriching my life is a spectacular understatement.

I wish everyone could be lucky enough to learn from Hao in the ways I have, and continue to.

I wish you could stand in a room filled with heart-rending music born of years of devotion to learning classical guitar and bamboo flute.

I wish you could be in the park on a foggy Wednesday morning following his impossibly slow and graceful Tai Chi movements, trying to match them breath for breath without falling over. I wish you could feel the delight of having him stop mid-form to point out the sudden appearance of a migrating cedar waxwing.

I wish you could witness Hao's kindness: the way he'll engage with a person whom everyone else ignores out of fear or convenience. Someone who turns out to be a fascinating, beautiful soul with a powerful story—just like him. Hao will never deny another being the dignity that he was denied for so many years; never let others be underestimated the way he often still is.

I wish you could sit in our writing circles and hear him read through tears his memories, his regrets, his longings. That you could witness the bottomless well of feeling, of deep love and excruciating loss, rendered simply as an offering of beauty, for which he wants no credit.

You may not get to do these things, but you do have this book.

So I invite you not only to enjoy it (you will), but also read closely, and watch how this person travels through life. Note how he relates, feels, acts and—most importantly—how he watches.

Notice how the author stands back, lets life come forward into his senses, and into his heart. How he's in no hurry to convey what he sees. How the observation is the inhale, and the expression is the exhale.

Notice how he is in conversation. The curiosity he brings. How so often, he chooses to say nothing at all.

Notice his kindness. The way he prioritizes dignity. The way he is with elders, with young people, with creatures.

Notice, too, the kindness he shows to himself, though not in any obvious or self-rewarding way. The writing of this book, for instance: the patient, methodical, and courageous way he has let these stories bubble up and flow out.

It's something that few others (if any) of his generation have been able to do, with a past that is so painful, so inexplicable, so very long ago.

Hao has broken his own heart again and again to let these stories flow through, so that we can learn from them, so that the truth doesn't die with his generation. Maybe it actually would have been kinder to himself *not* to do this, but his soul's calling prevailed.

As you'll read, racism prevented Hao from becoming the professor he wanted to be—and robbed countless aspiring scientists of that gift as well. Still, he has found ways to live from his teacher's soul.

So yes, make a study of this book. Move through it slowly, mindfully, breath by breath, knowing that you are in the presence of a great teacher. Someone who has somehow navigated this life—one full of more pain and challenges than most—with grace. Who has somehow found joy, who injects beauty into this world, and who, if we let him, will show us how to do the same.

Joy Reichart
July 2025

Introduction

Đường Xưa Lối Cũ is a song about returning to your home village, traveling down a dirt trail, listening to the sound of the bamboo flute in the air, watching the moon rise over the straw huts, longing for a mother who no longer lives and the girl you love who has left for a faraway place. It is a song that all Vietnamese of my generation know and love.

The Old Village Road is my personal Camino, my pilgrimage to regret, remember, and mourn. I return and walk every step back into the past to visit everyone, dead or alive. It is part of me and I will forever live with it.

This book is about Vietnam and my people. It's about an old man returning to Hanoi after six decades in exile to find his long-lost clan and walking the road that he and his brother had traveled as kids. It's about the survivors of bombing and defoliation, re-education camps and the new-economic zones. It's about boat people and refugee camps. It's about an old soldier afraid of the jungle. It's about a Việt Kiều looking back for a home he has lost, and songs he can't sing anymore.

It's about current environmental issues with the legacies of war, rapid human development, poverty, and the bleak future for poor farmers in the Mekong Delta as sea level continues to rise.

It's about people with trauma, with broken hearts and broken lives. I write because I see me in them, because I could be them, because I envy them, because I pity them.

This book also carries hope for the generations born after the war. Many of them are still stuck in the deep craters of the past. Some of them may be able to escape the legacy of their parents' suffering, environmental and humanitarian atrocities inflicted upon the people and the land. I wish them the very best.

I have asked myself about the reason and purpose for writing these stories and often I found the answer to be a search for understanding of grief and longing, the meaning of life and love, and the anger I still feel about what happened to us. I write to cleanse myself of the darkness that haunts me and hope that it will help bring peace to a place and people I love.

Since the publication of my first book *Skinny Woman in a Straw Hat* in May 2023 by Autonomous Press, I have thought that I had nothing left to write and yet there is more. The title of that book bears many meanings: the shape of Vietnam on the map, the love for my mother, and the resilience of the Vietnamese people. Again, the stories in this book are love letters to the skinny woman in a straw hat.

The Old Village Road

Má ơi, con về đây, Má ơi. Those were the first words I jotted in my journal as I was on the flight back to Vietnam to look for my mother and the family I had left behind. The English translation, *Mother, I am coming home*, was inadequate to capture what I could in my native tongue.

It had been twenty years since I left Vietnam as a young man to go overseas, a trip that should have been four years but it had turned out to be a journey around the world while I waited for the right time to come back home.

Let me just start from the moment I got off the plane at Tân Sơn Nhất airport and walked out into the crowd of Vietnamese people waiting outside behind the steel barricade that separated them from the rest of the world.

I always travel light. In the Jansport, I packed only a few essentials: a few clothes, toiletries, and three pairs of sox. Most important were my journal, the Canon camera and ten rolls of film. In a leather pouch hooked to my belt and inverted into my pants, I hid six envelops with 5 one-hundred-dollar bills in each to give to Ba, Má, and four brothers.

I strapped on my backpack and descended a metal staircase to the hot tarmac of Tân Sơn Nhất Airport. The tropical air hit me like a wet towel. A rusty bus took the throng of tired and nervous arrivals to the terminal only a few hundred yards from where the plane parked. Together with a couple of hundred tired and loud Việt Kiềus, I reentered a world I had long left behind.

After two hours in line to get my passport stamped and my backpack X-rayed by stone-faced officials, I was free to walk out through the gate. The sight shocked me as soon as I took the first step out the door. I thought I was confronting a mob at a political protest waving signs and screaming at the arrivers. They had waited for hours in the heat and mid-day sun but that was nothing compared to the years they had spent longing to see their loved ones again.

I too had waited a long time for this moment. I left Vietnam as a young man to go to college in Australia shortly before Saigon fell. I was among the lucky students who could leave for the safety of another country while the war raged on, killing and maiming people from both North and South. From afar, I followed the news of the weeks and months of intense fighting leading to the infamous *Giải Phóng*—the Fall of Saigon on April 30, 1975, fearful that I would never be able to go back home again.

Sometimes first love is not meant to last. Australia was kind to me but I didn't stay there long enough to finish my studies. I fell in love with Diep and she was the reason we ended up in America.

Now, I was coming back to Vietnam with an American passport and a tourist visa. I had lived overseas longer than the first 18 years of my life spent in this S-shaped coastal country in Southeast Asia that was my home once. Somehow, it scared me to set foot on it again; I had no idea what was beyond the barricade.

It was just a blur when I stepped into the blinding sun outside the airport. I fell into another world and drowned in a flood of memories. I could hardly breathe. Then I saw an old woman at the far edge of the crowd, her eyes locked with mine.

"Má?" I mumbled.

She ran and threw her arms around me. Her light bony body shook as I held her. She was a lot tinier than I remembered. I had grown and she had shrunk. She held my face with both her hands and looked in my eyes, traced the contour of my head and brushed my thinning hair. I didn't hear much of what she was saying, it was in a foreign language.

I heard many voices calling my childhood name, *Xê*, the French letter "C" for boy number 3, the third born of seven boys. I saw the dark faces of my brothers, the four who still live in Vietnam. They were now strangers with familiar eyes and crooked smiles. Their wives and kids had also been waiting for me in the midday sun.

I sat down on the hard pavement as they squatted around me. I passed out the four envelops to my brothers and they quickly stowed them away in their pockets, an act that resembled smuggling, something stealthy so no one else could notice. For me, it was a peace offering or an ask for forgiveness. For them, it was much needed as they were still hungry from many years since Giải Phóng. Five hundred dollars could feed a family of four for a year back then.

"We will go to my home first with Má and then the others will come for dinner." My brother Bê (B) told me.

I went with Bê and Má in a taxi cab to my old neighborhood in Gia Dinh. My other brothers escorted us for a while on their mopeds with their wives and babies. I felt like a hostage who had just been released and welcomed back into the protective arms of his home country.

Bê's house was a tiny one bedroom in a small alley. A sign above the entrance said: *Nhà Tình Nghĩa*, which I understood as a government gift to someone who had served in the Viet Cong resistance army for their sacrifice. I took it that it belonged to his wife's family.

Má kept her bony hand on my arm the whole time. She smelled of eucalyptus oil, her breathing was short and difficult.

"How is your asthma, Má?" I asked.

"The air is better at the farm," she said. "I only stay at Bê's house when I come to Saigon."

"Where is Ba? Is he alright?" I was eager to see my father. I heard he had served ten years in a labor camp up North and came back barely alive.

"Your father stayed back at the farm. He is still recovering from re-education for *Học Tập Cải Tạo*. Rest first, and you will see him in a few days." Her eyes never left me. "You are so much taller, heavier, and your receding hairline is just like him. Have you eaten?"

I said the airline had fed me. She told me to take a siesta and I lay down on the straw mat on the tiled floor next to her divan. She fanned the flies away, her breaths shallow and labored. I couldn't sleep in the heat and jet lag. My body was pumped full of adrenaline. My mind tried to believe that I was back in Saigon, back in the bosom of my family, back with Má. All the nerve endings were on fire, all senses alert and overloaded. I was a tiger in a new zoo, still figuring out the nooks and crannies of its new enclosure.

● ● ●

For dinner, Bê's wife had prepared a big pot of steamed rice, some mackerel stewed in fish sauce, Ong Choi fried in garlic, and a large bowl of pumpkin soup. The meal was a simple and classic Vietnamese dinner that I hadn't had for ages. The other three brothers came with containers of food they bought along the way: goat curry, Hunan chicken with rice, and half a roast duck. They laid it out on the tile floor where I was lying down to nap.

Bê was now the leader of the gang because he was the oldest of the four brothers in Vietnam. Of seven, I and two refugee brothers live in America. The four brothers in Vietnam had found their own ways to survive in the new regime after Giải Phóng.

"Let you change from those clothes. It's too hot here for that." Má made me take off my travel clothes and put on a T-shirt and shorts, just like my brothers.

I had trouble sitting cross-legged. There were not enough chairs in the tiny house and we sat on the cool tiled floor in a circle with the hot meal in the middle. My brothers laughed at my awkward shifting of the body to relieve the cramps. It had been too long since I sat in a lotus position.

"Your belly is in the way?" Brother Bê teased.

"It's not the belly. It's my back. I'm not used to stretching this way." I laughed with them.

"Just like the old days, eh?" Bê asked, passing chopsticks around.

"We used to fight with each other over rice, we fought for everything," I said.

Growing up with six brothers was brutal. We compared every morsel of food to make sure no one got cheated. Even with bananas from the same bunch, we made sure to hunt for the largest one.

I remembered the system of how justice was served: "Two, four, eight, even six is easy. Seven is tough but we perfected the art dividing everything by the odd number. The rule was the one whoever did the dividing had to pick last."

With so many hungry boys fighting over food, my eldest brother created rules for us to follow. He would be the one giving the signal during each meal—"Go!"—and each of us could reach out with our chopsticks to grab one bite of fish or chopped pork, stewed in fish sauce. Nobody moved until the next signal. When it came to rice, there was no signal and whoever finished their bowl could go for a second. We all tried to pack as much as possible in the first bowl. My brother Bê had a brilliant strategy. He always filled his first bowl half-full and was always the first one to finish. That way he was certain to get a full second helping.

"We didn't have rice to eat for so many years after you left. It is just beginning to get better now. You are lucky to come back at the right time." There was no hint of resentment in Bê's voice.

"I am sorry I wasn't here with you," I said as I tried to hold back tears.

"Welcome home, brother Xê," my brothers said, reaching out to touch me. "We are so glad you came home."

"One more story now that we have finished eating," Bê reminded me. "Before there was toilet paper? When we were little kids?" We all laughed at the most basic needs that I had forgotten.

Before there was any paper, my brothers and I always used water. It was water from the cistern that caught rain water from the tin roof, the water we used for bathing and cooking. It was also where I netted the mosquito larvae to feed my Betta fighting fish. The older always helped the younger. I asked one of my two older brothers to wash mine. The younger ones asked me and we were all glad to do the honor.

One would take a scoop of water from the cistern and pour over the bum of the crouching brother while rubbing between the cheeks with one foot. It was cool and smooth.

As we got older, we learned to clean our own bottoms ourselves. I still remember the newsprint, really rough paper that was used to wrap food, a few grams of pork belly or a piaster of onions and cilantro. Every week, Má burned the can of soiled paper as an offering to the gods.

We laughed about our regimented father and how he ruled with an iron fist: "Ba came home with rolls of soft tissues he got from his American friends. Proudly, he hung them on the bathroom wall—his handwritten note in charcoal said: *Fold in half, four squares each.*"

Slowly, I caught up with the strangers sitting around the circle. Bê had put on a slight belly and his thick hair had turned salt and pepper. For many years, he didn't have a job or a roof over his head. His luck turned after he met his wife whose family had land and was more connected with the new regime. She impressed me with her gentleness, a genuine kindness that came from the Mekong Delta. Their son was just one year old since they had him in their late thirties. Bê's hands shook a lot. "Malaria," he said with a grimace. He contracted it in Cambodia when he went there with the youth volunteers after the fall of Saigon. Since he had served and redeemed his sin as the son of a South Vietnam officer, he now could hold a trivial bureaucratic job.

The other brothers found unique skills I had never dreamt of. One had become a tailor and made a living sewing nice clothes made to order. One ran a farm in the new-economic zone near the border with Cambodia. The youngest brother worked for a sawmill and now ran his own business making and repairing saw blades. They all were married and had one toddler or two. Other than Bê who was one year older than me, the other three brothers were still kids when I left for Australia. Now, they were adults with families of their own, four strangers with oily hair and yellow teeth. Only their eyes and smiles reminded of their young selves and the rest I had just started to build like puzzles. I bet they didn't remember me well either.

"What happened to your hair?" one asked. I was the only one in the family who was balding.

"I don't know. Must be Bơ Sữa?" I meant butter and milk, the Vietnamese joke about rich people living well.

Nobody asked me about Australia or America. They didn't ask what I did to survive the first 10 years when I struggled to learn English, earn college degrees while washing dishes in restaurant kitchens, and what I was doing now for the U.S. federal government. I didn't know if I could tell them in any way for them to understand or relate to but thankfully, they never asked. There was no common frame of reference between us as our worlds were so far apart. I was just a half-American with enough money to give each a gift that could feed their families for one year.

● ● ●

The next day, Bê took me out on his Honda motorcycle. He merged into the Saigon traffic with me hanging on to his thin waist. He showed me the old neighborhood where we grew up. The Saigon of my youth was about a square mile around my high school, named streets and many numbered alleys, and a big open marketplace that sold live chickens, fish, shoes, and everything else. As if the market was not enough, street vendors carried their loads on their shoulders and squatted down with their baskets of fruits and vegetables along every sidewalk.

Tall African mahogany trees planted by the French a hundred years ago still lined the famous boulevards like cathedral columns. Towering tamarind trees with tiny confetti leaves shaded school yards and pagodas.

We drove through a forest of storefronts with gaudy signs, dusty street trees, and millions of people. Saigon had become another Bangkok, only poorer and dirtier. Everyone I knew still called the city Saigon although officially it was now Ho Chi Minh City. The air was unbreathable with rich exhaust from a million small engines. My ears were bombarded with constant blasting horns. After years of living in America, I had become used to the quiet and clean air with plenty of space to myself. Here, I could smell the next person's sweaty shirt, the cigarette smoke in their hair, and the fishy *Nước Mắm* odor on their skin. In this grimy and crowded city, everyone was going somewhere or doing something, buzzing like bees. An old part of me was awakening—everything I saw and heard was familiar yet totally new.

Bê stopped the bike and we took a couple of plastic seats at a Phở noodles stall across from a school. Little kids in blue and white uniforms arrived for classes.

"Remember your old high school?" He lit me a cigarette.

"Vaguely, but it has a new name. It used to be Hồ Ngọc Cẩn."

"They change the name since Giải Phóng and it is now an elementary school." He ordered two bowls of beef noodle soup. What it lacked in quantity and flavor was made up for with salt. I glanced into the courtyard where I had spent seven years of my youth before I graduated and left for good. Two large yellow signs with red letterings reminded me what I used to see every day: *Tiên Học Lễ, Hậu Học Văn*—first learn respect, then literature. What's new was the flagpole that flew a red flag with a yellow star instead of the three red stripes that my friends and I saluted to before class.

"Má always said you were a good student and held you up as an example for all of us." Bê reminded me.

"Before I was admitted to this school, I was bit by a dog. I still have the scar in the back of my leg." I showed it to Bê.

"Dog bite is lucky. Má kept saying that."

Unlike me, brother Bê was not studious, but he had the street smarts I have never developed. Like water, he would find the path of least resistance, while I was blind to the cracks in the rocks to flow through. I know he had been caught stealing little things, shocking to me as I had never thought I could. He bought comic books, read them, and sold them back to other kids, with a little profit to boot. He operated a mobile grocery store, selling any-thing he bought for ten piasters for twelve. In America, he could have been a successful businessman.

"Do you remember Má's business schemes? They never worked out," he laughed. "But she really tried."

"Yes, I know. She tried everything."

The year before I left Saigon, she got excited about a new plan: "Quail is the business to be in. Their eggs are selling very high." Má must have got the idea from the other women in the market. Indeed, there was a feverish trend in the country to raise quail for their eggs. It was advertised that quail eggs were good for health, better than chicken or duck.

She hired someone to convert our small kitchen area into a quail pen with rows of wooden boxes and chicken wire, stacked on top of each other like little condominiums. Then she ordered a few dozen baby quail from a Chinese supplier in Chợ Lớn. After two months, the quail reached maturity and the first eggs arrived—small, mottled and delicate. At first, prices were good, as there was a strong demand for them for Chinese noodle soups. After a few months, so many people were doing the same thing the market flooded with quail eggs. Má ended up feeding us the eggs she couldn't sell and eventually the skinny quail that she couldn't afford to keep alive. It was like that with her other ideas too. If someone showed her a shiny shovel she would reach for it. But the handle would always crack, or the spade would chip. She would end up with a hole and broken shovel. Somehow, she always kept on digging. It's the only thing she knew how to do.

In rare moments, I had seen her truly happy, bent over the old Singer sewing machine, making us shirts or pants. Her feet pushed the large pedal, her right hand on the flywheel, her eyes fixed on the needle going up and down. One time she learned how to bake at her sister's school of home economics and was so proud of the sponge cake she brought home to us. Later she brought home some burned cream puffs that came in different shapes and sizes, but they were delicious. She watched us eat with tears in her eyes.

"I can only feed you," she told me. "I don't know how else I can help you in this world. I can protect you for this long, but soon, I will have to trust the gods to care for you."

I, too, was afraid of dying young. I grew up during the war and saw death and dying around me. Friends went to war and didn't come home. I focused all my time and energy on school work because that's the only thing I was good at. Then one day, my fear of death was replaced by the fear of the unknown.

I was the first of my family to go to college, the first to leave home for a place thousands of miles away, the first to board a big jet plane to Singapore and then Sydney, Australia. I'd left Tân Sơn Nhất Airport one November afternoon after my 18th birthday. Through the airplane window, I'd seen squares of farmland, groves of coconut and banana plantations, thatched roofs, checkerboards of boulevards and a labyrinth of alleys. I tried to find my neighborhood but the plane had entered the bulbous clouds and burst into the blue sky above.

●●●

I went to the farm in Tay Ninh to see my father, the farm, and where Má had been living since Giải Phóng. Though it was only 100 km from Saigon, it took more than three hours to get to the town of Tay Ninh by mopeds. Má was on the back of Hòa's bike and I was with Bê. It was better to ride those little bikes than be packed in an old odorous bus with fifty sweaty people and no room to breathe. From Tay Ninh town, we turned West and followed a dirt road for another ten miles toward the village. Green paddies stretched out forever with Bà Den Mountain looming on our right side.

Hao Duoc village was what had become of the new-economic zone here. Two decades after the campaign to develop the jungle near Cambodia into agricultural farm land, the village was still a frontier of civilization. The roads were not paved and red dust covered every tree and thatched hut. We arrived at the farm by midday and turned into the gravel yard.

The main house had a dirt floor and the a few posts held up the thatched roof. A light bulb hung perilously in the middle. Má's room had a bamboo cot covered with a straw mat and a small cabinet held the only few clothes she had.

"I used to have a few old books to read but the termites ate them," she explained. "We just began to have electricity here, but we still need candles and kerosene lamps for the blackouts."

Hòa and his family lived in a room in the back. They cooked and bathed outdoors behind the banana plants.

"The toilet is outside. Make sure you don't fall in. But I got you a roll of toilet paper, just in case you forget how to use water." Hòa joked as he pointed out to me a pit shaded with palm fronds in the middle of the farm. "One day I will build an outhouse, but I am too busy right now."

Ba came out from his hut behind the cashew trees. He was in shorts, naked from the waist up showing off his ribcage. He gave me a toothless smile. I asked how he was and he laughed at the way I spoke Vietnamese with unnaturally clear pronunciation. "The American! The American!" He laughed.

We sat on the bamboo bench under the cashew tree. "How long are you going to stay?" He asked. "I am happy for you to be in America. You are the lucky one, and you have done a lot for this family."

For the first time ever, I recognized his voice, a blend of accents from Huế, Hội An, Danang, Saigon, and Hanoi, all mixed like a concoction of fish sauce with lemon juice, hot chili, garlic and sugar. But the amazing part was what I had never heard before, because I had never really listened. His voice was like a signature, the fingerprints of his life to identify where he came from and where he had lived.

He asked about my in-laws and about the relatives in America, and then he expressed his dim view of America: "There is no friendship between countries, only privileges. One day, America will have to pay for what happened here. There is a great debt they owe us."

I asked him about his years in prison camp up North and he said nothing. He shook his head, "Let's forget about it. Best to not look back. Nobody will thank you for remembering."

Suddenly, he grabbed my hand, "The old Seiko. It is still running. I told you, just keep it oiled every ten years." He had given me this watch before I left Saigon for Australia. His hobby was repairing broken watches he got from his army friends and this Seiko was his favorite.

I took a few portraits of him with my Canon as he admired its solid metal construction and bright clear glass. He liked gadgets so I let him use it for a while to take pictures of the farm.

I found Hòa in the yard changing the oil on his old Massey Ferguson tractor, a red workhorse leftover from President Diem's Rural Development campaign in the 60's. He waved his hand broadly across the hot dry landscape:

"This is *Kinh Tế Mới*. We came to this new-economic zone after Giải Phóng when I was 15. Má was the head of the household because Ba was sent to re-education camp. We cut down the large trees, built our own home with their timber, planted cashew, cassava, potato, and peanut. What you see is a lot better than years ago. Our brothers left this place one by one. Two went away and made it to America to join you. The rest found their way back to Saigon. I stayed because I had nothing better to do and now, I am a farmer. I own a lot of the land that nobody wanted and I will make it work with fruit trees. Mango maybe."

The sun was setting and it got a little cooler. Má came out to play with Hòa's two toddlers. She sat on an old piece of plywood in the yard spoon feeding the babies porridge from a bowl. The corners had worn off the plywood from years of decay and weathering. The veneers were delaminating like gaping mouths. It was the same plywood that Ba brought home from the American military base to make platform beds for my brothers and me. It had traveled with Má all these years and was a witness of my family history while I was away.

She saw me with my camera and smiled, a timeless image that I captured.

"Will you come with me to America?" I asked her.

"No, my dear son. I am too old now. I will be a burden to you. With a little money you give me, I can live here. It's a lot cheaper to live here."

She was not that old. At 64, she had already resigned to be too old for new adventures.

I sat with her and vowed that next time I came back, I would build her a house and that she would not worry about money anymore. She was just happy to see me and we stayed that way for a few more days before I left to go back to America.

She never asked questions about my life, the 20 years in Australia and America. I wonder if she already knew or that she knew that she could never really know. How could she ever know how much I missed her and home, and how long I had waited for the day to come back?

Rip Van Winkle fell asleep and woke up twenty years later. He even missed the American Revolution. The same thing happened to me. I had lost twenty years with my family and missed the fall of Saigon. I had not shared their lives and all they had been through since Giải Phóng. And here I was, sitting on a piece of plywood with my mother trying to fill in the blanks that I could never fill. I was glad that we had survived, all of us, and was happy with the old village road that I found, what was left of it.

Coogee Beach

"Come on mate! We will show you a great time," the old man said, his breath a mix of cigarette and beer.

I replied in textbook English, "No, thank you, sir."

"C'mon, young man. You will like us blokes. No worries, mate," he insisted, his big hand on my knee.

"I must get off soon," I said meekly.

"Don't. We have beer, mate, lots of beer."

I pulled on the chain. When the bus stopped at the next block, I got off.

"How are you, Hao?" Mrs. Cush greeted me with her usual cheerfulness, her arms around her little dog.

"I am fine, thank you. I was invited by some old men to go drink beer with them on the beach."

"Bloody bastards," she shook her head. "I saved you a lamb chop and mashed potato in the fridge."

She sat down in a big easy chair and watched the BBC news with the dog on her lap. I took the food downstairs to my room in the basement.

My small room in the walkout basement opened onto a square lawn that I mowed every Saturday as my contribution to the housekeeping. A rusty rotating clothes hanger twisted and squeaked noisily in the wind. The cold ocean winds whistled through leaky window sashes at night. In the outside world of black and white and shades of gray, the only object I saw in the dark sea was the lonely flat rock named Wedding Cake Island. Waves crashed over it leaving a constant frothy icing on top.

The summer of 1973 (in November that was), I arrived in Sydney with a cohort of 55 high school graduates from South Vietnam. We were selected by the Colombo Plan Program to be trained and returned to help the homeland that was devastated by a bloody and endless war. For the first three months, we were to be in "Prelim" together before being dispersed to universities across Australia. The program host had arranged for us to stay in dorms and rented houses in small groups. She said there was an Australian family willing to host one person and asked if anyone would be interested. I quickly raised my hand.

Mrs. Cush's little green house on Garnet Street perched on a cliff with an awesome view of the Tasman Sea. She lived alone with a yapping, smelly, long-haired mutt that slept in her bed. There was no Mr. Cush, just a B&W picture of a young man in uniform on the fireplace mantle. For room and board, I paid her fifteen dollars every fortnight with my allowance money from the Colombo Plan scholarship and still had another fifteen for pocket money. It was a very generous gift from the Australian Government to third world kids like me.

Back home, I was always surrounded by family and friends, but in that quiet suburb of Sydney, I found myself alone most of the time. I could not sleep no matter how hard I tried. My stomach growled constantly. I was a naïve kid from Saigon, a fledgling away from the watching eyes of my overprotective mother. I had never been on my own before, let alone in a foreign world.

Although I wanted to practice speaking English with her, Mrs. Cush wasn't much of a talker. Between feeding me and watching TV, I didn't know what she did with her time. Peter Cush, her older son, on the other hand, was quite a character. He came by once in a while to visit his Mum and always took the time to teach me Australian slang. "You're too formal," he commented. The Australian vocabulary according to Peter consisted of mostly "not bad, not too bad, and not bad at all." One of his favorite words was "entertaining." The rest of the time, he focused on helping me up my consumption of beer. He sang with a pewter mug raised high in the air.

"Two arms, two legs, two steely bands,
Under the Southern Cross we stand,
With a piece of wattle in my hand,
And more piss..."

He was also concerned about finding me a girlfriend. "First, you must gain some weight."

Putting on a few pounds was easy. I found Australian food very rich with plenty of meat and dairy. I loved the thick cream layer on top of the milk delivered daily to the house in quart-sized glass bottles. Before Australia, I had never tasted lamb because we didn't raise sheep in Vietnam. Now I ate lamb chops almost every week. The first time I bit into one of those, I could not stand the burned fat that smelled like body odor. I must admit though, it didn't take long for me to love lamb and I soon became addicted to it. Put a slab of raw meat on the grill with just a little salt, let it sear until the fat melts and drips into the flaming coal, and my gastric juices start to flow.

As I learned to drink beer and eat Australian foods, I went through withdrawal without the daily bowl of rice. Má used to boast to everyone how her seven sons could go through a kilo of rice each day. For each meal, she cooked a three-gallon pot and we ate it all to the last grain. The burnt rice at the bottom was the best part and we fought over it. With Ba's salary, he could only supply rice. The rest of our food came from Má's hustling in the market, and at times with money she borrowed from relatives.

"What would you like to eat, Hao?" Mrs. Cush asked as she sensed I had eaten enough lamb for the month. Besides broiling meats, Mrs. Cush cooked everything the English way and that involved boiling potatoes, carrots and peas mostly.

"Do you have any rice? I miss it."

"Hmmm, let me try," she said. "Bring some friends. I will make Asian food for you. How about this weekend?"

"I can make the rice for you. I know how to cook." I offered. She said no worries.

I invited Thao, my long-time friend from high school and Mai, the girl he liked. Thao was enjoying being in a dorm with many cohorts. Mai shared a flat above a grog shop with two other girls.

"How do you like your solitude?" Mai asked when she saw my basement room.

"It's quiet but I have time to study. Too lonely sometimes."

"You are missing out on ping-pong and volleyball," Thao said. He played every day with others in the dorm. "But the view is great here. It is really beautiful."

Dinner came, and Mrs. Cush really did her best. She boiled the rice too long and it turned out the same texture as mashed potato. We didn't say anything but she seemed to notice our reactions. Despite my encouragement, she never tried cooking it again.

● ● ●

Each day, I took the bus from Coogee to Randwick Technical College for English as a Second Language with my cohorts. We practiced listening comprehension in the language lab, conversations with Mrs. Moody, and building our scientific vocabulary in biology. It was intensive immersion in a new culture and we had to do it in a hurry before being thrown into classrooms to compete with Australians born and raised there.

One morning, I decided to walk to Randwick College to save the fifty cents bus fare. It took more than an hour to cross over the hills of Coogee and miles of the coastline dotted with palm trees and pencil pines. The Sydney summer sky hurt my eyes. Its ultra blue sunshine shone like the opal jewels that I saw in the David Jones department store. Everything about Australia was extraordinary compared to the smoky and noisy Saigon I had just escaped. Colorful cockatoos roosted in the street trees and city parks. The Eucalyptus trees with smooth blue trunks and leathery leaves oozed a strong fragrance of the oil Má used to ease her asthmatic breathing. Their shed bark and tough woody fruits crunched like roasted peanuts under my feet.

Back in Saigon, I always carried an identity card with my picture and date of birth. Any policeman could wave his baton to stop you in the street and demand to see my ID and whether I should be in the army already. In Sydney, I still carried an ID card in my wallet along with my Vietnamese passport, but no one ever asked to see them. Australia was a nation without worries about war, or a draft, or anything at all. I hardly saw any people in uniform. I never heard any explosions, near or far. It was deadly quiet.

If I could walk to school every day, I would save twenty dollars a month—about what my father made back home as a military officer. I sent the first twenty dollars back home over the Christmas holiday so my family could have more food for Tết. Má wrote, "Dear son, please don't worry about us. You need to take care of yourself first. I wish I could cook for you. I miss you very much."

I kept sending money home, twenty dollars every three months. Twenty Australian dollars could feed a family in Vietnam for a month but was only enough for my bus fare. I wondered why Vietnamese were so poor while Australians owned houses with rose gardens and drove new cars without toiling in the hot sun?

Peter loved to tell me about the Australian value of hard work. "Don't work too hard, mate." He would expand on it over a beer. "This is the lucky country. Do you understand? We have a large continent, lots of natural resources, and few people. Welcome to the land of wonder, down under!"

Regardless of Peter's advice "no worries, mate," I had no choice. Many of my Vietnamese cohorts came from the same poor background and we all tried to save money by sharing food and rent. My friend Thao and I often shared our lunch, half a sandwich each. The ham and cheese sandwich from the Randwick cafeteria tasted bland but the red apple was delicious. It was crispy with a flavor that I had not found in mangoes or pineapples. Tropical fruits overpower you with sweetness but apples seduce you.

I was gaining weight so fast I needed new clothes. My friends and I went to the downtown outlet stores to buy bell-bottom jeans and tee shirts. We all bought the discounted clothes in the same colors, white, red, or blue, and we ended up in uniform. All the boys grew their hair long to be like the Hippies. Thao even wore a white headband that became his trademark. At Randwick, we stuck together like a bunch of crows. Despite the cold stares from the locals, we squawked in our native language, played badminton and ping pong during breaks, and smoked cigarettes in the yard.

I had trouble making a few sounds that were completely alien in my native tongue. For example, the "J" in words like June and judge. That hard J sound is a harshness not found in Vietnamese. The most difficult sound for me was the "Th" sound in The, This, That, There, and Then. We spent hours practicing this. Mrs. Moody told us to put the tongue between our front teeth and draw it back, quickly, like Th… is. I tried but it always came out funny, sounding like De or Te. Most of us gave up and just said, "Duh."

After two months in Sydney, I had a dream. In it, I was living, speaking, and thinking in English. Before that, I was still dreaming in Vietnamese. I realized then that my immersion into another culture had officially begun.

•••

In Prelim, a young person's thoughts also turned to Love. Of the 55 students that came with me from Vietnam, only a third of them were girls. At first, they were ordinary looking. These smart girls had pimples and wore thick glasses. I would never fall in love with any of them, or so I thought at first. After hanging together for a month, they started to grow on me. Somehow, they looked fuller, fleshier, perkier, and downright sexy. I was longing for a companion to remind me of home, someone who could cook with *Nước Mắm* and speak Vietnamese with a Saigon accent. I found that all the guys in my class were undergoing the same lustful transformation. Since there were twice as many boys as girls, a kind of competition began, and a cheesy soap opera ensued. We started to pay close attention to who talked to whom and who was invited to the next party.

Mai was among the most popular girls and she was blooming like an Australian Waratah flower—suddenly in full glorious display. She waited for me after class and asked, "How did you do? Did you get what they said on the tape?" I shook my head and said, "Chị (sister) Mai, I failed. I couldn't understand much of it."

I had failed my first English test with a score of only 20 percent. I thought my English was good enough since I earned a Colombo Plan Scholarship to leave Vietnam with the best students in the whole country but I was wrong. Back home, I had learned English with Titus Peachey, a Mennonite missionary in Vietnam. He taught me well but I was not prepared for this kind of English—words like Fairdinkum and fast slurring sentences ending with "Mate." Maybe I needed many more months of training with Peter Cush, and many more beers.

Mai and I walked through the Eucalyptus scented campus. I didn't have much to say when she finally asked, "Would you like to come to our house this weekend? The girls are cooking spring rolls and beef noodle soup."

I lit up and said, "Yes, thank you. I will be there."

Thao was also invited and he must have felt very hopeful that she liked him too. He talked to me a lot about Mai so, out of respect for a long-time friend, I kept away from her. I was extremely shy around women, growing up with all brothers under the close watch of my mother.

The weekend came. The girls had found rice noodles and ingredients to make a Vietnamese feast. They had to substitute a few herbs and spices that they couldn't find in Sydney. There were some Chinese grocery stores then, in the early 1970s, but they didn't carry Vietnamese ingredients. Someone got hold of a bottle of *Nước Mắm* in a care package from home and that bottle was worth its weight in uranium. All my fellow students drooled over it. There was no sauce on earth like fish sauce, especially when you were hungry, and, skimping on meals as much as I could, I was hungry a lot. Thao and I bought a six pack of Foster's Lager that looked like oil cans.

There was not enough furniture in this rented house for a dozen of us. Dinner was served on a blanket spread out in the middle of the living room. We squatted and huddled around the boiling pot of fish, tomatoes, celery and fish sauce. The girls made egg rolls with ground pork, mushroom, shredded carrots and onions wrapped in wonton wraps instead of the traditional rice paper. It didn't matter. It was delicious.

Thao picked a strategic position right next to Mai. Other boys jockeyed for positions as the night went on. A few had already had too much to drink and started to sing songs and quote poetry. I kept myself distant from Mai and paced myself with the beer. Across the room, I noticed Mai's eyes on me the whole evening. I avoided her gaze but I could feel the back of my neck tingle, that instinct that we have when being watched.

"Did you see the listing of where we are going?" Mai asked the group after dinner. "Yes." Of course, we did. After three months of Prelim at Randwick College, the cohort would not be together anymore. We would get sent off to different cities: Brisbane, Melbourne, Adelaide, Perth, Hobart, and Canberra, depending on our chosen fields. The Colombo Plan managers wanted us to have separate experiences and opportunities to assimilate, not to bunch up together and party among ourselves on weekends.

Thao told us, "I am staying here to attend the University of New South Wales. Many of us will stay because the college of mechanical engineering here is the best."

I knew I was heading to Canberra, the least desirable city of all. As the capital of Australia, it was an artificial city built to settle the rivalry between Sydney and Melbourne. Someone told me—probably a joke—that Canberra is an aboriginal word for the place between two breasts: there is not much there to see. I had heard that only a handful of Vietnamese students had ever gone there. The city itself was very small and home to the federal government, international embassies, the Australian National University and not much else. The university was best known for political science and forestry. I was sent to Canberra because I chose forestry as my major.

"You lucky guy. I wish I were going to Canberra," Thao said with sad eyes.

"Why, my friend? I am being exiled to the most boring place on earth. You can play ping pong and volleyball here in New South Wales with the engineering gang. I will be dancing with kangaroos."

"Mai is taking political science," Thao said.

Reality set in. I realized Mai and I were the only two in the group going to Canberra.

Mai came over and sat with Thao and me. In a month we would be separated. When would we be together again? Mai began to cry. Thao almost reached out to comfort her. I tried not to move a muscle.

"Anh Thao, I will miss you a lot," Mai said. "You have been very kind to me and I am glad for you to stay in Sydney. It is a beautiful city, the most beautiful harbor I have ever seen. It will always be my first love. I wish I could stay here."

"Then change your major. It is not too late," Thao said.

"No, I don't want to be another engineer or computer scientist. I want to learn how good governments work and the political systems that make other countries strong. I want to see Vietnam as clean as Singapore, as productive as Japan. I long to see that day." Then she changed the subject, "What about you Anh Hao, why forestry? Nobody in our group even thought of that. You are a loner and weird."

"I don't know what I am doing but it seems so romantic," I said, unsure of my word choice.

"Yes, it is really romantic! Being outdoors among the trees, sleeping under the stars with mosquitoes, wading in wetlands with leeches," she teased.

"No, like you, I want to change something. Our Vietnam has been destroyed by war, Agent Orange, and government corruption. Our forests are mostly destroyed and the rest will be cut and sold in time. Someone has to restore them. I will go back, you know?"

The three of us sat in silence. We were young and naïve, idealistic, hopeful and afraid. We didn't know back then that we would venture out in different directions and travel far beyond our youthful plans. None of my cohort went back home to live in Vietnam after finishing college. After the fall of Saigon, many became Australian citizens and some, like me, left for the U.S. or Europe to reunite with their refugee families. Many became successful engineers, teachers and business owners. The Colombo Plan did not accomplish its objective of preparing us for post-war restoration for Vietnam, but Australia and the world gained hundreds of well-educated citizens. All the dreams I had back then to return and restore a ravaged land never happened. I am no longer a citizen of Vietnam and would not have any influence on its future.

The year 2004, I returned to Australia for a reunion with my friends. Thao took me to Coogee Beach for a visit "down memory lane." Thirty years after I left Sydney, the house on Garnet Street still looked the same but with a different shade of green paint. I knocked on the door and asked the owner if the Cushes still lived there. The lady said that the house had been sold many times and she didn't know anything to tell me.

For a while, I stood on the cliff of Coogee and looked out to the sea to search for something familiar. Under the opal sky, waves still crashed over Wedding Cake Island, leaving a frothy icing on the lonely flat rock.

My American Journey

My friend Tai invited me and my wife Diep to take us on a road trip with him across the country. Since his escape from Saigon, he had settled in the U.S. as a permanent resident. "I met a gorgeous girl in the refugee camp and she lives in Houston now. Let's stop there on the way." We said yes. Why not?

Tai's green Plymouth Duster had an engine powerful enough to launch a space shuttle and we reached the Texas border within three days with hardly any rest. Without money for hotels, we just took short naps in the car and kept on driving. Hurtling at ninety miles an hour on the open highway was easy. Then blue lights flashed behind us. We pulled over to the gravel shoulder.

A big trooper in cowboy hat and sunglasses studied us through the car window. "Show me your license and registration."

Tai reluctantly complied. "What's the matter, Officer?"

He took his time looking at Tai's driver's license. "Who are you kids? Where from?"

"We are students. Just visiting friends in Houston." Tai tried his brave face. I didn't like any of this. Diep woke up from her deep sleep in the back seat, her eyes round like a racoon's.

"You were speeding, way over. You may spend the night in jail." He kept looking at the paperwork.

I tried to think of what to do or say and found our situation hopeless. Just three skinny Asian kids in a car in the middle of nowhere with Texas law enforcement.

"Are you Chinese?" he asked.

"No, we are from Vietnam. Refugees," I said, overstating my immigration status.

"Hmmm, my people fought there, died there, maimed there. All for nothing. And now, you people are here taking over our country."

I didn't know what to say. Not much to say when you are in a hostage situation.

"You are the first ones I have seen on this highway. Now, get the hell out of here." He gave back Tai's papers, tapped on the roof of the car and then walked away.

● ● ●

My American journey began fifty years ago when my wife Diep and I entered this country legally from Australia and became illegal aliens for overstaying our tourist visas. Our immigrant story was rather unusual, at least for most Vietnamese refugees who fled South Vietnam when the Communist regime overtook Saigon on the "Liberation" day of Giải Phóng in April 1975. We were students in Canberra and were crazy in love. She decided to stay behind with me when her family left Australia for America. Her father's job at the South Vietnam embassy in Canberra was no more and he needed to start his life all over.

She still reminds me often, "If I went away with my family to America, we may have never seen each other again. We would always be in love and remember only the best of each other."

One year after our small wedding in Canberra without families on either side, we spent all our savings on airplane tickets to visit her parents in San Francisco. After a couple of weeks of our stay in their apartment in the Sunset district, her father convinced us that we should apply for asylum status like most Vietnamese refugees and we should qualify. I reluctantly did, knowing I would have to give up the Colombo Plan scholarship that had scooped me from Vietnam and trained me for the last three years and with one more to go. However, this was my chance to give back to Diep for her having stayed by me.

Every six months while our status was pending, we received letters denying our petition, with the threat of deportation even though we could not be deported anywhere. There was no way we could be deported to Vietnam because the war was just over and refugees were fleeing like rats off a burning ship. Back home, my family was persecuted because of our background with the South Vietnam army. My father was sentenced to life with a slim chance of parole in a jungle reeducation camp up north. Má and my young brothers were banished to the new-economic zone near the Cambodian border. We couldn't be deported to Australia either, because we were not Australian citizens and could not return to Canberra once our temporary passports expired.

While our petition for asylum was pending, we lived in a limbo state they call "parole," meaning not here or there, and it went on for years. I washed dishes in restaurants and Diep waited tables for relatives and friends of her family. I took every gig that

I could find in the back of the newspaper: delivering phone books, mowing lawns, shelving tires in warehouses, mostly for a week or two.

I tried to continue my education by taking a few classes at the City College in San Francisco because it was almost free. I could barely afford the tuition to pursue the degree in Forestry at UC Berkeley, but I wanted so badly to accomplish the goal I set when I left Vietnam many years earlier. I can't recall how I did it, but I knew it took everything I had and then some from Diep.

A recruiter from Weyerhaeuser Company came to the campus and after an interview, I landed an internship for the summer of 1979. I was to report to their Technology Center in Washington State. In our old Chevy Vega, Diep and I drove up Highway 5 through Northern California, Oregon, and then to Seattle. We found a place to share with an old Vietnamese man in Tacoma. Every day, I drove to work at the Tech Center in Federal Way, a bit north of Tacoma.

Weyco sent me with my boss Len Mahoney to work at Craig, the company's MDF (Medium Density Fiberboard) plant in Oklahoma. Going to Craig for three weeks in August was an assignment nobody else wanted.

Diep came along for the trip. We were young, adventurous, and eager to learn everything about America.

The hot air hit me in the face as we stepped off the plane in Dallas. Len rented a black Lincoln Continental and we drove for a couple of hours through endless Southern Pine plantations to Broken Bow, Oklahoma. We checked into the motel, the only one there.

Broken Bow was a small southern town with a few shops downtown and two traffic lights. The only entertainment was the drive-in theater in a big empty lot. Big oak trees lined every road, very picturesque if you can ignore the heat. All I had heard about the town from other company employees was true: You either work at the Craig mill or the chicken farms. There was nothing else there. At least the MDF mill might smell better.

"Are you Choctaw?" the pizza shop woman asked Diep when she bought two slices.

"No, we are Vietnamese."

"Viet-Manese? Sorry. You two are the first ones here."

After twenty years of sending American people and weapons to Vietnam, some people still couldn't spell or say it right.

For a treat, Len took us to a steakhouse in Texarkana one Saturday night. Say what you want about the atrocious summer weather in the South, the beef was to die for. Diep enjoyed a thick and juicy T-bone while I devoured a bloody serving of rare prime rib, downed with a large beer. Len just enjoyed watching us eat. On the way back in the dark against the backdrop of the pine plantations, we saw a procession of people dressed in white sheets.

"Look! The KKK are having a party," Len chuckled.

"What's that?" Diep and I didn't know then what KKK meant.

"Ku Klux Klan. They don't care much for foreigners." Len kept the Lincoln Continental steady down the dark and empty highway, back to Broken Bow. "I hope you will take over my job soon. I am going to retire in a couple of years. They need someone to do QA/QC at Craig."

After the summer internship with Weyerhaeuser Company, I learned everything about MDF. I truly enjoyed working and living in the beautiful Northwest and was hopeful to get a permanent job with the company after graduation, even though it meant having to return to Craig many more times. But that didn't happen.

When I graduated a year later, I was still waiting for my asylum petition to be approved. I applied for a permanent job with Weyerhaeuser company, but they could not hire me because I had no permanent resident status. Because I was undocumented and unemployable, I had no choice but to continue to stay in school. By the time I was granted a green card and then citizenship five years after, I had earned a PhD and was way overqualified for most regular jobs.

Throughout the graduate program at Berkeley, I believed that I was destined to be a professor. I maintained a 3.8 grade point average and my research project with Professor Brink was cutting edge. He was best known in the field of wood chemistry and processing.

Upon graduation in 1986, I began to apply for teaching jobs, starting with the Dominican College, a Catholic school in Marin County, God's Country, in the North Bay. The nuns invited me over for an interview and I drove there in my only tweed jacket, a white shirt and tie. Walking through the beautiful campus, I felt like a Choctaw again. I was probably the first Vietnamese to ever set foot on this beautiful part of the San Francisco Bay.

I gave a lecture on water chemistry, pH, and acidity. Maybe I overdid it, trying too hard to explain the negative power of base-10 logarithm of the hydrogen ion concentration in aqueous solutions. It was too much math and I should have picked a simpler topic. When I finished, the nuns had tears in their eyes.

I got a rejection letter a week later, "We wish you success in your research career." It sounded kind and sincere, as if I were just too brilliant a scientist for the teaching job at their college.

Next, I applied for all Assistant Professorship positions advertised in the back pages of professional magazines: *Organic*

Chemistry, Chemical Engineering, Forestry, Pulp and Paper, and *Wood Science and Technology*. They were looking for graduates with my expertise. I sent transcripts and letters of recommendation by Dr. Brink to Oregon State University, University of Maine, Washington State, and more. All sent back prompt and standard rejection letters without any offer for an interview. There was no explanation or feedback.

Other foreign students told me that it was impossible for them to get into academia because of the perception that they don't have the communication skills to teach. Having a name like mine didn't help.

Once I gave up the dream to teach, I turned to the wood industry. Weyerhaeuser Company was downsizing so they were not hiring research scientists. Other forest products companies did the same after decades of clearcutting in the West. Sawmills were closing down everywhere. Furniture manufacturing in the East had started to be outsourced to China, timber to Canada, pulp and paper to Brazil.

A position as a Research Scientist in the U.S. Forest Products Laboratory in Madison, Wisconsin got my interest. Hailed as the crown jewel of the Forest Service, the Lab is a world-class research organization dedicated to conservation through wise use of wood since 1910. Everything from lumber properties, structural designs, and pulp and paper technology came from it.

An Assistant Director of the Lab came to Berkeley to interview me and one week later, I got a call from the Project Leader offering me the job in the Fire Research Unit.

"I understand you are hot stuff," she joked. "You come highly recommended."

Diep and I packed everything we had in our car and drove two thousand miles through the beautiful Rocky Mountains and the

Great Plains to the Midwest. We arrived in Madison on July 4th, in time for the fireworks followed by tornado warnings.

It didn't take me long to become an expert in fire research. I completed the literature search for all scientific publications in combustion, ignition, heat and smoke release, charring of wood, and all the test methods used in fire science. I burned everything from small wood samples to large structures in experiments to understand how wood ignites and burns in order to improve the safety of buildings. The Fire Lab was the hobby shop for a pyromaniac, and it kept me warm through six long winters in Wisconsin.

The Midwest people were nice and kind, but Diep and I found ourselves alone and isolated. Every long and icy winter, we felt lonely and cut off from the warmth of family and friends, and the familiar food that we could only get with a three-hour drive to the Vietnamese refugee quarter in Chicago.

After six years in fire research, I jumped at the chance to move to the Forest Service Headquarters in Washington, D.C. My research peers joked, "He got burned out." They gave me a big farewell party to say goodbye to the firebug.

Working and living in the nation's capital, I broadened my view and awareness of the people and land management issues in the country. I gained a clear understanding of how the government works, and the more I knew, the deeper my cynicism grew.

The way the system works is a subtle kind of deep-rooted corruption. Every Department was created to serve specific interest groups. The Department of Commerce supports oil companies, and of course, concrete and steel. The USDA subsidizes corn, soybean, dairy, and many more "stakeholders." The Forest Service is not exempt and even with the noble mission to "care for the land and serve people," its primary purpose was in support of timber production, mining, ranching, and recreation for rich people, for decades. My previous fire research work at the Lab was to help the wood industry protect their market share.

The thing is, the general public doesn't have a voice or a face. As a public servant, I should have been working on what's best for the public but I never heard from them. Most people I know don't have a clue how the government works and the people who know don't want to tell them.

The legislative branch of the government turned out to be much more corrupt than the executive side. For leadership training, I spent six months as a Legis Fellow on Capitol Hill, part of a Brookings Institute program to learn how Congress works. I accepted an offer from a Senator's Office to help their staff with forestry issues. Western States such as Idaho, Colorado, Utah, and Montana represented the way America used to be. With populations mostly in rural areas, their agendas were "dig deep, drive Jeep, eat meat, and something to do with sheep."

I realized then it's no fun to work on the Hill unless you can take sides.

I am apolitical by nature and being a federal government employee forbade me from participating in partisan politics in my official capacity. Although my role on the Hill was to provide technical expertise, the Senate office accused me of being a liberal. A staffer picked on me for being a Berkeley graduate. "That explains it!" she laughed.

"Bring us only the science that we can use," said the senior staffer. He didn't like what I had to say about the new ecosystem management approach in the Forest Service.

After twelve years at the Forest Service headquarters in DC, I asked to be reassigned to a management job in California, closer to the research projects on the ground and of course, closer to family in the San Francisco Bay Area. I was happy to be away from politics and enjoyed the remaining twenty years of public service in the field.

After a long career, I retired at the highest level as a member of the elite Senior Executive Service. I have been to all fifty states and a few territories and done more things in this country than most Americans. I have all the rights of a citizen by birth except one: to be President. As if being an immigrant, I am less qualified.

• • •

My relationship with America is ambivalent at best, and hypocritical at worst. In America, I represent the model minority, the classic success story of an immigrant who came with nothing, endured the initial hardship and abuse, and achieved the proverbial American dream. I love this country for all its natural beauty and the many kind hearted people I have come across, and yet I can't help feeling a deep-seated resentment for all the deaths and destruction it has inflicted on the people and place that was my first home.

The America I saw as a Vietnamese kid was a country of great firepower, helicopters in the air, and convoys rumbling through our streets. I was 10 years old when my father took the family to China Beach to see an air show. This was the year 1965 when the U.S. involvement in Vietnam started to escalate, and the exercise was to show off the military might America was bringing to the region.

Out in the open sea, plane after plane dove and dropped real bombs on the water. Explosions deafened my child ears. Water columns rose and splattered like mushrooms. The air reeked of gunpowder and the acrid smoke from burned napalm choked my lungs. Machine guns from the airships must have killed all the fish; if they were not directly hit, the pressure from bomb explosions blasted them to the surface. Shock and awe. I knew then at that tender age what America was about to do to my home country.

When I returned to the Mekong Delta twenty years after living overseas, I broke down crying at the sight of skeletal coastal mangrove forests destroyed by Agent Orange. Veterans told me that these toxic chemicals were applied on them to clear vegetation for miles around army bases. Worse yet, more of the spraying was on rice fields to deprive the people of food supplies. The persistent toxins still linger in the soil, causing mysterious diseases and premature deaths.

I still mourn the sufferings and deaths of millions of people, from both North and South, over twenty years of a bloody war and for decades after, not to mention tens of thousands of lost souls from America and allied countries. My heart aches every time I see footage of napalm bombs blooming over the rice fields. I couldn't bear the pain when I read accounts of the My Lai massacre of hundreds of villagers, women and children included. For years, I couldn't watch a war movie or read a book about Vietnam. I am still moved to tears when I hear an old song in my language, words I remember but can't sing anymore.

No matter how American I have tried to become, I am reminded of who I am by strangers who tell me where to go. One day, I was in Maryland on the way to fish the Pennsylvania limestone creeks. When I pulled into a station to get gas, an off-duty policeman had been following me. He was still in uniform but without the gun and badge. I was filling my tank when he walked right up to me and took a look at my license plate.

"Why don't you get your ass back to Virginia." Then he walked away. I could still smell his hot breath. At least, he was kind enough not to say out loud that I should go back to my country.

I have heard that line many times and it always caught me cold. I didn't know what to say. Maybe I was just too stunned to think of a comeback answer. Maybe I still don't know which country to call home.

My late father-in-law used the Latin verse "Ubi Panis Ibi Patria" to justify loyalty to his adopted country. To me, bread alone is not enough to make a place my home. I wish I could say that I have found a permanent home here, but my heart doesn't tell me so.

Refugee Camp

I arrived at St. Luis Reservoir on a hot August afternoon, excited to see my brother and his friends for a three-day camping trip. After living for six years in Wisconsin and another twelve in Virginia, I had now moved back to California for good. This camping trip would be a chance to reconnect with him.

The sun was going down over the golden California hills, their ridges streaked with green oaks. I had driven along Blood Alley, the famous stretch of Highway 152 connecting 101 with I-5, past the famous Casa de Fruta, joining big trucks rolling down steep grades. The hill on this side of the valley never saw much rain and grew mostly grass. All the moisture had been squeezed out of the air as it traveled over the coastal range, long before it reached the valley.

The reservoir welcomed me with its blue mirror surface that complemented the golden hills. I turned left at the Reservoir Recreation Area sign into the campground where my brother and a hundred others held their annual event every first weekend in August. The elderly ranger handed me a sticker for the parking lot. "Are you joining the Vietnamese camp? Your friends are waiting for you," he said with a smile.

I drove down to the campsite. There were at least thirty cars in the parking area. Nearby, dozens of family-sized tents had been erected under the few lonely pine and sycamore trees. Barbecue smoke permeated the air—lemongrass chicken. This was going to be a different camping experience, not the solitude that I was used to as a trained forester.

I found my brother sitting in front of Ed's large tent. It was set up like a tavern, complete with a green Heineken sign and a neon red "OPEN" sign. Ed's tent was the watering hole for all to stop over for a beer and a smoke and seek relief from the 90-plus degree heat.

"Have a beer!" My brother stuck a can of Budweiser in my hand as soon as I sat down on the canvas chair next to him. The cold liquid went down easily after three hours of driving an old Toyota Camry with very low freon pressure. I shook hands with Âu, the chief planner for the camp, and exchanged a few grunts with a dozen men sitting in a semicircle facing the lake. My brother had amassed a large number of friends who had served in the South Vietnam army and now lived in Silicon Valley. They rode the wave of the booming tech industry and, after years of hard work and frugal lifestyles, live comfortably in homes they own and send their kids to private school. He invited me into his circle of friends and of course, their annual camping event.

● ● ●

My brother is three years older than me and the eldest of seven boys. The year before I left for Australia, he joined the South Vietnam army. He had finished two years of college and then had to enlist. "We didn't bribe them," he later told me about his lack of options. He signed up to serve with the elite Air Force. "It is better to be shot out of the sky than to die in the jungle somewhere." He went to basic training for six months and every time he came home on leave, he was a bit darker, tougher, and more taciturn. He took me out for *Phở* one day and then lit me a cigarette, the first one I ever smoked. It was nasty, bitter, hot, and made me gag, but I tried to brave it for my oldest brother. I wanted to be his friend. I knew he and his friends went "down village," a few dark streets that were well known by all the kids in my class. I used to ride my bike home from school late at night through down village and the women in white blouses and black pantaloons would call out from their doorways, "Young man, come in here. It's the same everywhere!" I always sped up to get out of there.

I also heard the joke about the "rocket," the big tube of penicillin injection you need after going down village. "When you are going to die in battle, maybe tomorrow, who cares?" my brother explained. Maybe it is natural. Men get horny when they face mortality, just like pine trees producing massive amounts of pinecones when facing a drought.

As the oldest, he played the Lion King role with the rest of us. Although I was three years younger, I was already catching up with him in size. One time we were just boxing around for fun and I must have got him mad with my jabs—he punched me in the nose with a straight shot, real hard. I bled and, from then on, I quit challenging him. Although he wanted to show us who was boss, he never cared for the responsibility placed upon him as the first-born son. "It is all bullshit," he said. "All those Confucian ideas were to impose social order. I don't buy it. I can't do anything for Mom and Dad, and I haven't done much for you guys."

Then we didn't see each other for a long time. I left Vietnam the year before the fall of Saigon while he went to Alabama for training with the U.S. Air Force, part of the Vietnamization plan to teach Vietnamese to fight the American way: with technology and fire power. Like real friends, we exchanged letters about our respective lives in foreign lands, my school progress in Canberra and his adventures with women around his base. "They are like Perdue chicken, all meat, and very soft," he wrote. After six months of good living in America, he went back home just in time for the most hellish time of his life. After the fall of Saigon, the new regime locked him up in a re-education camp for one year. Because he didn't have much of a chance to engage in combat, his sentence was relatively short. The real punishment afterwards, however, was much more deadly. With a bad family history of military men, our father especially, he would never be allowed to work in any office or go back to college. In Vietnam, that meant you would be doomed to a life of hard labor.

He told me about his years after Giải Phóng. Each day, he was with the army of men and women combing through the steamy mountains of garbage for plastic and metals, anything that could be salvaged and recycled.

"I made the most money selling the soil beneath the landfill. It was the richest fertilizer. You just have to dig deep enough through the stink."

He and his friends took turns pedaling a heavy *Xe Ba Bánh*, a three-wheeled cycle designed with a flatbed in the front. They hauled loads of bananas to the markets or bricks to construction sites. His transport work and the landfill job kept him alive for a few years.

"You don't know what *đói* is," he said, recalling the hunger. "If I could only count on a full meal each month, I could keep on going. I kept dreaming of a good day, with some meat and maybe a beer."

Every few months, I sent a care package home and he was the one to receive it for the family. He made sure the yard of black cloth went to Má, the vitamins to my younger brothers, and sold the odds and ends to buy food. I always made sure to include a carton of Marlboro for him to smoke and sell in the black market, in singles. He also asked me to include a package of B&W Kodak photographic paper, eight by ten, to sell to photographers to sustain their portrait photo business.

•••

"Dinner is ready!" Âu shouted as he rode his bicycle around the camp. "*Bà Con ơi!* Dinner is ready!"

The crowd converged on the main shelter. Two lines formed and moved steadily through the mess hall. First, a server put a tennis ball size scoop of rice noodle in your bowl, a second server poured the hot broth in with a chunk of pork hock and a few slices of cooked beef, then a third server sprinkled spring onion and cilantro on top. I added shredded *Rau Muống*, the morning glory greens that Vietnamese could not live without. The *Bún Bò Huế* beef bone broth was flavored with bunches of lemongrass and copious hot chili pepper, all enriched with pork hocks. It has always been my favorite noodle soup because it reminds me of my father's birthplace. The soup was so spicy it made my brows sweat and eyes water. They say that you need to cry to remember the old capital of *Huế* when you eat *Bún Bò*.

Once through, we carried the steaming bowls and chopsticks across camp and slurped our soup down in small groups. After the first course, everyone went back to the mess hall for a dessert of sweet mung bean *Chè*. Hot tea and instant coffee were available 24 hours a day and people helped themselves, at will.

This ritual would go on, three full meals a day for the long weekend. I was eating better at this camp than I did at home! They had been planning this camping trip at the desolate St. Luis Reservoir the whole year, emailing each other about the logistics of feeding 100 people for three days—menus, recipes, how many pounds of meat and vegetables to bring, propane stoves, large pots, spoons and chopsticks.

Âu and company planned this annual event with military precision, starting with booking the entire campground. They booked both large campsites, A and B, to make sure they had the whole park to themselves and no other campers could complain about their fragrant cooking, smoking, and late-night noise. That meant that both campsites had to be reserved exactly at the moment the online booking went live. My brother and Âu were in charge of this logistical step. As soon as the booking site went live at midnight on April 1st, they already had the data for A and B pre-populated on two separate computers and just had to hit submit simultaneously. Once both campsites were booked, emails went out to all 100 members that the gig was on and then the planning committees could take over. They took these extra measures to reserve the whole campground but they never had much competition. No one else wanted to be there during the hot and dry month of August. For these Vietnamese campers, it was the perfect venue.

After dinner, another team went about cleaning up and taking the bags of garbage out to the dumpsters in the parking lot. It took only half an hour before the mess hall was clean and ready for another round the next day.

It was getting late and the women retired to their tents with the young ones. It had been a long and fun-filled day in the sun.

• • •

The men huddled at a long concrete table to smoke cigarettes and drink beer as night fell. My brother and his friends had intended to stay up all night. It was going to be a *Đêm Không Ngủ*, an entire night of marathon storytelling and singing that I used to have with friends. The last one I had was when I said goodbye to them before I left for Australia.

The women had been thoughtful enough to leave out on the table an array of roasted peanuts, beef jerky, and pickled radishes and carrots to complement the beer. Just about everyone lit up, as most Vietnamese men still smoked. Some had quit but made exceptions on this night. The sky was a dark void dotted with stars and the lake surface smooth as glass. The whole landscape was bathed in moonlight. I realized why they chose this reservoir location year after year. It was like sitting on a beach and looking out over the ocean. The temperature was also perfect, not blazing hot like before, but not cold enough to need a campfire.

Ed brought out his collection of tequila—beautiful bottles of clear liquid.

"OK! Now you are talking!" my brother cried with delight.

"This is for you guys—my brothers. I love you all. I wish we had won that war though," Ed admitted. He was among the last Americans to leave Vietnam. He tried to save all the refugees that he could but was ordered by his brass to stop flying back for more. The U.S. could only stick around the coast to rescue boat people and those last refugees who could reach the aircraft carrier by helicopter. Ed came home with no hero's welcome and a bad case of guilt about the buddies he left behind.

"I am sorry I couldn't do more. You guys were left there to starve and die because of us. We let you down. We just quit," Ed said as he cut up a few limes into thin slices.

"We were willing to fight to the end but our leadership failed us," my brother replied as he puffed on a cigarette. "They fled first and abandoned us. We ran out of ammunition. Without American backup, we just dropped our weapons and ran."

I was in Australia when Saigon fell and witnessed the chaos and panic from afar. I worried about Mom and Dad and all my brothers. I wished they could flee and come to live with me but they didn't. I was the only one at the drinking table who wasn't a veteran or a real refugee. I was also a guest for the first time, having been away from California for two decades, and still trying to merge into my brother's circle of friends. I wanted so much to hear their stories.

The topic quickly turned to the last days of South Vietnam and how each person escaped. Some flew out in helicopters, some climbed onto ships. Others, like my brother, couldn't flee and endured years of punishment before finally escaping to sea in leaky boats.

"I was still a cadet, fresh out of military school. I never shot at anyone," my brother said. "I flew a couple of flights and then got grounded because we ran out of parts for the helicopters. Americans taught us to fight the war the rich man's way, with overwhelming firepower and modern equipment. They pretty much plowed the ground with artillery and napalm before they sent us in to mop up. The other side didn't fight that way. Their guerrilla warfare was low tech, but deadly and demoralizing. It was a sad ending for South Vietnam when President Nixon announced the Vietnamization process to pass all the fighting to us. We knew we were going to lose when America walked away."

"I am sorry, my friends," Ed said again. "I thought that we were winning. We had powerful weapons and air superiority. We could have bombed the North to submission, but we didn't. Our people back home wouldn't stand for it." Ed was apologetic. "Then we just quit. We lost."

"Our fathers were military, we were military," said Âu. "We were scum to the new regime and supposed to die off. I don't know how we survived, but we did. Maybe we were young, maybe just by sheer will, maybe the hunger drove us to do the impossible."

That's when my brother and his friends made a life-or-death decision to escape. They pooled their money, joined a group of other ex-military men and hired someone to find a boat. They waited in the U-Minh jungle for months before they snuck out to sea in the middle of the night. I had seen the U-Minh on one of my trips to the Mekong and it was a perfect hiding place. The U.S. bombed and sprayed that jungle many times with Agent Orange to drive out the Viet Cong but the trees wouldn't die. Their bark survived and sprouted back thicker than before, just like the resistance forces.

"The mosquitoes there had teeth," my brother added as he filled my little tequila glass. "I touched blood everywhere they bit. It was said that even the buffaloes needed mosquito nets."

My brother looked at me with his dark eyes, "We snuck through checkpoints and gathered at the rendezvous place to board the boat. Sometimes, we got shot at and ran like rats. It was dangerous to get through the Viet Cong coast guard in the dark but the horror really began when you got out to sea. The boat motor died within two days, and we drifted without power for another ten. You realize how big the ocean is and how small we are in the little wooden boat and all you see is water around and stars above. You pray not to die of thirst and hunger before seeing land again."

"It is just pure luck that we drifted toward Malaysia and got rescued by their fishermen. I kissed the ground when we landed on Palau Bidong," Âu said.

"I am sorry my brothers, we just lost the damn war. We abandoned you," Ed repeated. The tequila was turning him into a man of very few words.

"Funny thing is if we didn't lose, we wouldn't be here," said Âu. "Maybe they did us a favor, huh?"

Ed cut up more lime, emptied his glass down his throat, licked the salty lime off the back of his hand and exhaled, "AAHHH." He passed the drinks down the table, one round and then another.

"Where is the guitar?" my brother asked me. I opened my black case and pulled out the old *Guitarras Finas* I usually brought on the road. You only need to know a few chords to accompany Vietnamese music and I can play them well enough. After all, most of the songs we knew were all in the key of A minor.

"OK. Tonight is Bolero night—Boleros only," Âu requested.

"Of course, only authentic Vietnamese songs, nothing else," the group agreed.

The Vietnamese of our generation have adopted the boleros as our music. The lyrics of the sixties and seventies written to the boleros somehow captured two decades of our youth, loaded with longings for peace and home, regrets and loss, all rolled into the songs we still remember.

My brother started singing and others joined in. One song described a soldier in the foggy night in the central highlands, leaning on his rifle thinking of his mother, missing his village and longing to see his woman. In another song, a seafarer imagines the white foam in his boat's wake as nameless wildflowers that he wants to bring home to his bride. The rhythmic bolero beats played with guitar nylon strings were drowned out by the drunk voices of old men. It was magic in the night.

"You know? We used to party like this in Pulau Bidong," Âu said with a hint of sarcasm. "Oh! The beautiful island of Bidong!"

I was curious about this famous refugee camp near Malaysia. I asked, "What was it like?"

"Anh Hao, you are the lucky one to be spared of all this refugee camp stuff," Âu said. "That year, there must have been forty thousand refugees living on that one square mile island. It had enough space for a few thousand, at best, but there were too many refugees."

"Each family had a hut that we built from scrap wood and tin pieces, just to keep the rain out. There wasn't enough land to bury our waste so the island constantly smelled like shit," my brother said. "It was a beautiful island with sandy beaches but we ruined it. We must have killed all the nearby coral with raw sewage."

"We were prisoners on the island. Many people waited for years. Babies were born there, many people died there," Âu said.

"What did people do on the island? How did they pass the time?" I asked.

My brother said, "We took English classes, planted community gardens, organized social activities, ran our own hospitals, and spent lots of time in the mess halls. We cooked for hundreds every meal, three times a day. I brewed my own wine, really bad stuff. The food was horrible too. The Red Cross gave us shipments of instant noodles, SPAM, and mackerel once a week. That was our entire menu."

"How many ways can you cook mackerel? It smelled bloody no matter what, and it stank worse after days without refrigeration," Âu said, making a face. "I can never look at another mackerel again as long as I live. At least with SPAM you can stew it in fish sauce. A little bit goes a long way with rice."

"The food was awful but the worst part was the torture of the mind," my brother said. "Many refugees had been robbed and raped. Some were suicidal. We found ourselves alive but stripped of identity and dignity. We worried for our family, we missed our friends, not knowing whether they lived or died. We had no plans, no money, nothing. But you know, we were glad we survived the worst."

"How come nobody wrote stories about these experiences?" I asked.

"Nobody was thinking about anything but how to get off the island," Âu said. "There were a few poems written on rocks and gravestones, but they must have been erased by the rain and wind."

"Who wants to read about our lives? War, death, sorrows and loss? Nobody will thank you for that. Maybe best to forget," my brother said.

"I am the lucky one," I confessed. "I was a refugee too, I lost my family, I was alone and homesick for years. The difference is I never had to risk my life or go hungry."

"Brother Hao, you were our lifeline," my brother said, his arm around me. "You always did all you could to help us at home. I remember things you sent every other month—a yard of cloth for Mom, needles and threads, bottles of aspirin, a carton of Marlboro for me, things I could sell on the black market to buy food. Then you bailed us out of Bidong. Without you, I wouldn't be here now."

He lit me a cigarette. It was warm, rich, and full of colors.

"Enough about Bidong, let's sing boleros," Âu said. "How about *Những Dồi Hoa Sim?*" Of course, everybody knew the song, the *Hills of Ficus Flowers*. I strummed my guitar and they all sang the story of a soldier returning home to find his young sister dead. He was supposed to die, not her. The hills of the pink flowers that she loved were in full bloom but she was no longer there.

We sang songs about the flares floating in the night sky like red bright suns lighting the road home, the road of sorrows, the road of sufferings. We sang about love. We sang about home. We sang and sang.

I drank and sang with them. Our songs brought us back to a time decades ago when we were young and our country was torn apart. I got a glimpse into a part of my brother's life that I didn't know, the punishment he got for being on the wrong side, his escape, the refugee camp, mackerel and SPAM. The moon rose high above the St. Luis Reservoir and the lake reflected all its silver back to the sky. The park shelter lit up like a jewel in the dark. The breeze turned cold but nobody seemed to mind. For one weekend, they allowed themselves to relive a life that they had long tried to forget. They asked me to play one more bolero before going to their tents to sleep off the tequila. I picked the one that my brother and I had learned by heart when we were kids, the song about a young man saying goodbye to his girl before going off to war.

We sat side by side one night
The quiet moon lit our hair
A star sparkled in your eyes
Looking into mine
I whispered: in a thousand years
Your eyes still shine bright.

The Cranes Have Returned

We arrived at Tràm Chim Park at midday after a grueling four-hour drive. The further from Saigon (now Ho Chi Minh City), the worse the roads got, full of potholes and sometimes half missing. Most of the bridges over the canals and rivers were bombed out. We got off the van whenever the driver slowed down and went around the car-sized holes being filled with rocks and gravel the workers carried on their backs. Regardless of the treacherous roads, and the 90 plus degree heat, I enjoyed the green landscapes of farms, rice fields, and fish ponds everywhere I looked.

"Welcome to the Plain of Reeds," Dr. Kiet, Botany professor from Ho Chi Minh University and our in-country host, announced as we pulled up to the guest house, the only two-story concrete building that loomed over the bone-dry landscape of Tràm Chim Park. It was the end of February and there hadn't been a drop of rain for months.

"The Plain of Reeds, as the French named it, is a wetland ecosystem in the remote Đồng Tháp province," Dr. Kiet said. "Only one meter above sea level, the landscape alternates between dry and inundated depending on the season. It is the dry season now but in another few months, most of the park will be flooded with torrential rain."

"Đồng Tháp province is among the poorest areas in Vietnam," he continued. "During the war, the U.S. bombed and defoliated the entire area to deprive the Viet Cong of their hiding places. The fields were drained and burned, the earth scorched and the water turned acidic. Nothing grew for years. No trees, no birds, no fish. Twenty years after Giải Phóng, the fall of Saigon and the end of the Vietnam war, the land began to heal and the Melaleuca forest grew back. And the cranes have returned."

"Vietnamese people love cranes. It took years of planning and negotiation but, finally, a few thousand hectares of land were set aside as the protected wintering ground for the cranes, to ensure they never get exiled again."

Gordon, Deb, Harold, and I unloaded our gear from the van and mounted the steps to the second floor of the guest house. The four of us planned a trip to the park as part of a mission for the International Crane Foundation. Gordon, a wetland ecologist, led the team. Deb, his wife and my coworker, was a communications director in the Forest Service. Harold was a friend of ours who loved to travel, and I, a native speaker, was their de facto translator. Our mission was to spend a couple of weeks at the park to study the cranes' habitat but mostly to understand the needs of the local people.

Although the building was recently constructed, the yellowish limestone wash on the guest house had already turned moldy grey from the high humidity. Cobwebs covered every corner, making it easy for geckos to feed on the pesky, bloodthirsty mosquitoes. It took me no time to recall the clicking sounds the geckos made, "Chkkkkk chkkk…" The ground floor of the guest house hosted a suite of offices with the largest room at the end doubling as both the conference room and the dining room. On the roof, a flat observation deck provided a three-sixty view of the park to the west, and the village to the east.

Right away, Gordon and Deb hauled their tripods and scopes up to the top deck and set them up to survey the park. Harold chuckled as he and I followed, "I'm no birder, Hao. I came for the food."

The afternoon sun cast a red glow on the village like a classic Vietnamese painting: bamboo hedges and coconut trees encircling clusters of thatched roofs. In the park, cranes fed on fields of brown sedges and wild rice. Nearby, patches of Melaleuca trees stood out like throw rugs.

"Wow!" Gordon exclaimed. Deb echoed him, "Double wow." Even Harold pointed his binoculars to hundreds of cranes digging for water chestnut with their sharp long beaks. From afar, they looked like a herd of dinosaurs in *Jurassic Park*. "These are Eastern Sarus Crane," Dr. Kiet explained. "They are the largest among the fifteen crane species in the world. As tall as we are. Wingspan about six feet. They have grey plumage with a bright red cap and upper neck. Their body design is typical of wetland birds, with long legs to wade and long necks to stretch above the tall grass to watch out for predators. They are a threatened species and running out of habitat in Southeast Asia. This place is among the last set aside for them before they become endangered."

Gordon proceeded to give us the basic rundown on the crane's dietary and habitat needs, then he got to the good stuff: "They dance. Different dances. And they sing, actually they bugle." He pulled out a chart to show us different postures the cranes make. "They flap their huge wings to challenge rivals, jump acrobatically to attract a female, and stand erect with beaks pointed to the sky to bugle in unison."

• • •

The aroma of fried fish and grilled meat filled the air. In the court-yard next to the guest house, a few men sat around smoking and watching children hit a volleyball back and forth over a net. To the far end of the compound next to the bamboo hedges stood the workers' quarters, small concrete boxes roofed with corrugated steel like a military barrack.

The sun had set and there was nothing else to do but eat and sleep. Hung, the staff manager who spoke a little English, called out to us, "Dinner is served!"

The dining room was sparsely decorated with photographs of cranes and one large portrait of Hồ Chí Minh with his white goatee and knowing smile. Under the picture was the obligatory quote: *Nothing is more precious than independence and freedom.* The electric fans did little to keep us cool or disorient the hungry mosquitoes. By now, we simply resorted to using DEET to keep our ankles from more welts and hoped that the Lariam would keep us safe from Malaria. A feast was laid out before us: fish, pork, chicken, fried tofu, stuffed bitter melon soup and a big pot of rice. It was enough for twenty people. A woman poured tea and scooped rice into our bowls. She seemed to be about my age and dressed in peasant clothing. I asked for her name. "Hạnh," she said quietly and shrunk back, almost disappearing into the wall.

Hung pulled out a large bottle of Saigon beer and filled our glasses. "Don't worry," he assured us. "The ice is made with boiled water."

For a poor province in the Delta, I didn't expect to see so much food on the table. My friends were very happy with the roasted chicken and chunks of fried sweet potato. I enjoyed the bitter melon soup so much I had seconds. Má used to make a soup like this every time I was sick. She believed that the bitter melon was a good medicine to fight the common cold. The ground pork mixed with chopped onion, black mushroom and vermicelli stuffed in the hollow shell of the melon was a perfect combination of bitter and sweet.

"You didn't eat the broiled chicken," Hạnh later observed.

"I prefer vegetables," I told her. "I don't eat much meat."

For our following meals, along with the usual spread of grilled meats, I saw boiled potato leaves and stir-fried pea shoots with our feasts, along with a fish sauce dip, perfectly blended with ground chili and garlic.

Harold and I shared a room. We slept in wooden beds covered with flimsy straw mats, and mosquito nets over the top of us. At night, the air turned more humid, thickening to its saturation point. Above the humming electric fans, geckos sang their laments. "They say: fuck you, fuck you," Harold chuckled.

"I think geckos are just happy to sing to each other."

"Hey, she likes you, what's her name again?" Harold didn't miss anything.

"Her name is Hạnh. Good night, Harold. I should warn you I am famous for my snoring."

"Me too," he said. "If I can't sleep, I can talk to the geckos."

•••

The roosters woke me up the next day even before sunlight beamed through the vents. Gordon and Deb had already gone out birding with Hung and Dr. Kiet. Two things I learned about birders: they carry expensive gear and they get up very early.

Hạnh had breakfast ready when the team returned from the field in their muddy boots. "So cool! We got real close shots of the cranes from the blinds," Deb said, all smiles.

After breakfast of fried eggs and French baguette, we took a boat tour around the park. Very carefully, we climbed on the long and tippy wooden boat in the canal near the guest house. The boatman pull-started the motor and off we went. Gordon and Deb sat in front with their long lenses in their laps. With the humming motor behind us, we entered the protected area of the Plain of Reeds passing patches of Melaleuca forests, fields of water lilies and thick carpets of wild rice. Herons, egrets, and kingfishers took off ahead of us as we cruised along the waterway.

At every turn in the canal, I saw a rickety guard house and a couple of men squatting on the bank waving at us. Some were fishing with long bamboo poles. Dr. Kiet explained, "These guards are local people. Their main job is to keep poachers out. They help protect the trees, the fish, and wildlife."

We waved at the guards and they smiled back.

"This park is the last remnant of habitat for the cranes," Dr. Kiet reminded us. He made a wide sweep with his arm. "Without the park, where will the birds go to winter? The villagers want more land to grow rice, gather firewood, and fish. Conservationists like us want to set aside the land for the survival of the cranes. Everyone wants a slice of it for their needs but this park is small enough as it is. The key to sustainability of Tràm Chim Park is to improve life for the villagers. If they go hungry, the park is no more."

"What about ecotourism?" Deb asked, turning around to look at Dr. Kiet. "This beautiful place should be a real destination."

"That's what I am also afraid of," Dr. Kiet replied. "There is a limited amount of tourism that the park can withstand. Too much of it will destroy the habitat and will not serve the primary purpose of being a sanctuary for biodiversity."

Pham Duy's love song for the land, *Quê Hương Tôi,* played in my mind as I immersed myself in the Plain of Reeds. The poetic words of "My Homeland" paint a picture of village life, with wooden boats going up and down small canals. The wind carries the fragrance of golden rice fields and children's laughter in the air. An aging mother waits by the bamboo hedges for your return. The young girl's shy smile captures your heart and soul.

Every day, we toured the park in the morning and went to the local school in the afternoon. Most dwellings in the village were small huts with a few wood or bamboo poles to hold up their thatched roofs. Many of them jutted over the canals. Many villagers cooked and bathed with the same water they defecated in. All the natural resources they could find were small timber from the Melaleuca and bamboo. The small fish in the canals supplemented their diets. With the acidic soil, they could grow one rice crop a year, at best.

At the village school, we donated notebooks and pencils to the kids, along with two microscopes for their lab. My friends gave a few lectures and I translated for them. Gordon talked about wetland ecology and Deb told stories about life in America. The kids listened respectfully without asking any questions. In Vietnam, students never raise their hands. I wasn't sure how much of what we did helped them, but they thanked us for the gifts we donated.

I don't know how much of a difference we made, if any, but it felt good to meet with the locals. Environmentalism is a luxury of the rich and us Americans were the rich in REI shirts and Vasque boots among the poor and undernourished folks. The villagers seemed to appreciate that we showed up to spend time with them.

Sometimes we just played tourists and visited roadside stores, sitting at wood tables in straw huts with the midday heat beating down on the dry and dusty landscape. Hammocks stretched between posts invited us to take siestas. A mother hen walked around with her chicks picking up bits of dropped rice. A shy girl in a black tunic approached Hung and he made a chopping sign. She went to the side of the hut, hacked off green coconut shells with a machete and stuck a straw in each one for us.

Often groups of giggling children came in to check us out, their faces and hair covered in red dust. They liked to touch Gordon's hairy arms and look through Deb's Canon viewfinder. Soon enough, a dozen of them followed us around, laughing and chattering. The women in the market place nearby stopped their business to watch their kids and the strangers play. Older people managed a friendly smile.

● ● ●

One Sunday, I could not fall asleep during the midday siesta, so I walked around the guest house complex. As I rounded the cistern, I saw Hạnh squatting on the concrete pad washing dishes. I froze, not knowing whether I had invaded her privacy. She looked up and after a moment of hesitation, flashed me a smile. I nodded politely to acknowledge her and she laughed out loud at my manners.

"You are a strange man," she said. I took it as a sign that she wanted to talk.

"Chị Hạnh, how so?" I asked. Chị is how you address an older sister in Vietnam.

"You are so polite. Nobody around here is. They are Vietnamese. You are not." I was taken aback by this last line.

"I am Vietnamese," I said.

"No, you are a Việt Kiều. You are American Vietnamese," she said, shaking her head.

"How do you know?" I challenged her.

"You look different, you talk different, you seem lost."

I have heard that from others, even in America, that I always look lost. I wasn't sure what to say next.

"Do you like the food here?" She asked to break the silence.

"Yes, thank you. But why so much meat?"

"Anh Hao, don't you see? Your group pays twenty dollars a day each to stay at the guest house and eat three meals a day. That is plenty of money for here, so what you don't eat, the whole staff can finish. Your visit is good for everyone. They like the chicken very much," she said with a smile. I was glad to hear we weren't wasting the leftover food from our feasts. I saw a bunch of bananas hanging on the side of the kitchen, so I asked for one. She broke off a couple and handed them to me.

I got a bit bolder and asked her a personal question. "Chi Hạnh, tell me. Are you from here?"

"No, I am not from here. Most villagers are not from here. We are landless refugees who came here because we had nowhere else to go. This poor province is the end of the earth, but we have no choice. How about you? What is it like in America?" She shook her hands dry. There was no towel for her to use.

"America is a huge country. Life is easier there and even though I work hard, it is nothing like here. Americans are very lucky people."

"Aren't you lonely? Being so far away from home." This surprised me. Most Vietnamese would only ask invasive questions: How old are you? Are you married? How many kids? How much do you make? And, in my case, what do you do with all that money? I had been refusing to answer these questions whenever they came up but Hạnh only asked if I felt alone in America.

"Yes." Now we were having a conversation. "I was homesick for a long time. I missed my family and everything about Vietnam. This is my first time back after twenty years."

"You are a brave man." She stood up. "To go out there alone, learning a new language, living among strangers."

"What about you?" I deflected the attention back to her. "Tell me more about your life. Where are you from?"

"I grew up in the Delta. My parents were freedom fighters and fought against the French. They hid in the U-Minh forests for years and died there. I was adopted by the communist party and grew up doing everything they asked of me. I mean everything. I went from place to place but here is where they want me for now."

Suddenly, I realized that I was talking to a former Viet Cong, the enemy of the South and the U.S. If caught, she could have been tortured and killed. We were killing them and they were killing us. It was war and people became monsters to each other. Across from me now, she was no different from any villager I know—poor and kind.

"Next time you come back, I may not be here anymore," she said while looking down to avoid eye contact with me.

"Thank you for the bananas, and the bitter melon soup," I didn't know what else to say. I should have thanked her for being a friend, for talking with me and telling me her story, but it all seemed inappropriate at the time.

"Goodbye, Anh Hao. Please come back. Everyone here loves you." She looked up at me very briefly and turned away. I saw her walk back across the yard and disappear behind the kitchen.

● ● ●

To thank the staff, I gave Hung a hundred bucks to go buy beer and treat them to a big dinner. About twenty people came to the farewell party, all men. Hung thanked us for coming to help the people and the cranes. "Thanks to Uncle Ho and the Party." Every Vietnamese official always starts with this line. "The cranes are coming back. They had stayed away for a long time because of the war. Also, let's celebrate our friends from America and your coming home, Anh Hao."

He waved his hand to signal the meal to be served. Soon after the chopsticks made their first contact with the food, beer was passed around. The more beer we drank, the louder the party got. Each person had to make a toast so that they could all drink more beer. They would chant "Một Hai Ba Dzô!" every time someone made a toast, sang a song or cited poetry. Then more beer.

I noticed that Hạnh was not there that night. I thought she was in the kitchen frying egg rolls and making papaya salads, but she wasn't. When I asked Hung what happened to her, he answered, "She has been reassigned to another province."

That night after the party, Gordon gathered us for a debriefing. Something wasn't right.

"I need your help," Gordon said. His brow furrowed as he looked at me. "The boatman slipped me a letter and I need your translation."

I read the letter out loud, "I am Tuan, your boat driver. I am accused of stealing the motor, which is now missing. The park director demands payment of $700 or I will be fired, or put in jail. I am not guilty. Please help."

"What are we supposed to do?" Harold began. "Talk to the director? Doesn't sound like it's our business."

"No, it's really not our business," Gordon agreed. "It's their internal affairs. We represent the International Crane Foundation, and we are only visitors here."

"We should try and do something for him," Deb chimed in.

I tried to make sense of this theft, "If Tuan was not guilty of the crime, he didn't deserve to be fired. If he was, he had sabotaged his own livelihood, unless it was part of a scheme to escape from this place with some cash. Regardless, we would never know."

We had no idea what to do. If we did nothing, he would be fired. We could chip in for $700, he would still be fired. If we wanted to intervene by talking to the park director, what would we say?

We ultimately did nothing and I have never found out what happened to Tuan. Just like our goodwill mission, we came to help, but I am not sure we did any good. There is a saying among NGOs, "The ground is littered with failed projects." The problem is that well-meaning foreigners try to help with their ideas and money but they come and go, often without lasting impact. For real progress and long-lasting change to happen, the leadership has to come from within the local community.

● ● ●

The night before we left to go back to Saigon, I sat on a canal levee with Hung to keep him company while he conducted a crane count. I asked him how he counted all those birds. He smiled and said it wasn't that accurate, "You count groups of five or ten, and add up the number of groups."

Against the sunset, I watched the countless, dark silhouettes of those magnificent birds with their heads held high, steam rising from their beaks as they bugled. I didn't know what they signaled with their loud calls that carried over the green fields. They had traveled far on the power of their own wings and hearts, with a compass that never lost its bearing. They will continue making their annual trip to Tràm Chim to rest for as long as the land here welcomes them. They belong to a world without boundaries but their survival is delicate. For these migrants, their hearts are divided, and they call both places home.

The guard house across from the canal came into focus in the darkening landscape. A kerosene lamp flickered through the bamboo windows. Cooking smoke drifted from the house in my direction carrying a pungent smell of burned fish sauce along with Vietnamese *Vọng Cổ* music playing from a radio. I had never liked Vọng Cổ when I grew up here. Literally, Vọng Cổ means nostalgia and every song has the same rhythm and melodies accompanied with sad lyrics. Sitting on that canal levee, I listened to the song. It told the story of a young girl who left her village and ventured into the big city to live among strangers. She missed her mother, the rice fields, straw huts, and bamboo hedges. She missed the canals with little boats going up and down, and the egrets that came home at night. The music lamented the fate of people like Hạnh, whose life was as fickle as the water hyacinth drifting in the river. At that moment, that song was also about me.

Soon, I would leave the Mekong Delta and return to the comfort of my home in the U.S. I would leave the Plain of Reeds and this Melaleuca forest for the big sky and faraway places. But like the cranes, I would always find my way back.

Red Mud

Mai squatted on the hot dusty sidewalk behind two rattan baskets full of cooked sweet rice and banana leaves. Every morning, she set up her mobile stall under a large tamarind tree a few feet from the curb to sell breakfast food to people on the way to work. In her late thirties, her thick head of hair had already turned gray, covered by the conical straw hat that hid most of her face.

In front of her, an army of noisy motorbikes fired their engines in short bursts like a million lawnmowers running at the same time. The city was waking up fast and everyone had somewhere to go. The bikers squeezed together elbow to elbow, pushed and shoved their way forward, filling every available inch in downtown Ho Chi Minh City. Traffic lights turned green every minute, but no one moved. The city's arteries were clogged. Bikers stared straight ahead, holding onto their handlebars ready to surge forward whenever there was a gap. They were mostly young people born after the war: the men dressed in tailor-made white shirts and dark pants; the women donned dust masks and kept their knees together below short skirts—their legs covered in white panty hose to protect them from the tropical sun.

Mai tuned out the street noise completely. She silenced all of her senses—she felt nothing, numb. A few people stopped their bikes, leaned over and shoved money in her face. She scooped some sweet rice in a piece of banana leaf and handed it back without eye contact, without knowing or caring who it was. She put the dirty money in her right-side pocket, occasionally pulling out the mess of bills to sort them in some order, then continued to stare ahead at a spot about nine feet in front of her.

It was the day before Tết and soon Mai would travel home to spend a few days with her family. She would join the exodus of workers out of this city. These choked streets would soon be deserted; shops closed; work stopped. It was Tết. Tết is the time to return to the village to reunite with family and burn incense offerings to the dead. Mai had already bought presents: a kerosene burner, dolls, and a few bras and pairs of shoes, hard things to find in the village.

The policeman was harassing her again. He yelled and waved his baton, "You can't sit here! Move! Move!" She knew she was not allowed to work there, but everyone did. Where else? Half the city made a living in the streets. She tidied up her wares and put everything back in the two rattan baskets. With no eye contact with the man, she walked away with the baskets hanging over the ends of the bouncing bamboo stick. The load felt familiar resting in an exact spot on her shoulder. It bounced with her steps, up and down, up and down. She searched for the next place to put the baskets down and continue her business until the next policeman came.

She usually sold all her rice by midmorning and then prepared her next baskets of food to sell in the afternoon. Near Tết, she made money with mangoes. Rich or poor, people needed a couple pieces of perfect fruit to place on the altar. Mangoes were popular. They are the fruit of the gods, at least for Tết. She would leave for her village after selling the last batch of mangoes before they went soft.

●●●

Mai finally boarded a rusty old bus full of westward bound travelers. She shut out the loud yelling, body odor, bad breath, and cigarette smoke radiating from the driver and all the other men on the bus. With the windows open, the hot breeze embraced her and the passing green fields hypnotized her. The blaring Vietnamese Vọng Cổ music helped dull the senses too. It's always the same mournful tune with different sad lyrics about lost love and being far away from home.

Every time she traveled this road, she saw a bike crushed and someone sitting nearby holding their bleeding head. People stopped and gawked without helping the injured. One time she saw a body wrapped in a straw mat left on the side of the road. Nobody claimed it.

After three hours, the bus reached her stop. From the bus stop, Mai had another fifteen miles to go to reach the farm. She waved to a skinny man atop a bike. He smiled, flicked away his cigarette and kick-started his engine. For the equivalent of a dollar, he would take her to the farm. The road to the farm was paved now. Many years ago, it was a dirt road that turned to red mud every time it rained. It stuck to everything, clung to wheels, clogged engines, and held the villagers hostage. Along the road, different shades of green spread out far beyond the horizon. Banana plants and coconut palms grew on the levees around rice paddies and farmers' houses. The earth was hot and steamy during these dry months before the rainy season came.

Mai was only a few miles from home and yet her heart was heavy. Tết still stirred in her the echoes of her youth, an innocent time to play, eat, and visit with everyone in the clan. It was the best time of the year, the most restful, the most joyous, the most exciting. For one week, life should be happy if the gods were kind, rewarding them for their hard work. So was the Tết Mai remembered from her childhood, but Tết hadn't been the same since she left the village to live alone in the city.

She eyed the road with a sense of awe. Only fifteen miles and it seemed to run on forever, straight west, straight to Cambodia, straight to hell. It was the road she wanted to return to, yet whenever she came back she was afraid of it, as if it were haunted by ghosts, as if something would jump out from the field and pull her in. She had decided a long time ago to run away from it but she had to come back every Tết because it was where her mother and her brother lived. She would rather be a street vendor in the big city because she couldn't live in the village anymore, having to look at this road.

She lost her baby on this dirt road. It was raining hard. She was holding on to Dan, not yet one year old. The boy hadn't been eating. He couldn't keep anything down and the diarrhea was non-stop. Her husband strained to keep the bicycle from falling over, with Mai and the baby on the back seat. He leaned with all his weight on one pedal at a time, moving a couple of feet with every push. They had to get to the hospital in the next town, the only one nearby. The fifteen miles was endless in complete darkness. Only the sound of rain and bullfrogs kept them company. The baby was quiet, eerily quiet. The couple was sweating, pushing and pushing, foot by foot, mile by mile.

The doctors told Mai the baby could have been saved had he been brought to the hospital days sooner. Dysentery was a common killer in this part of the country, along with malaria or tuberculosis. He was a beautiful baby, a healthy handsome boy.

• • •

Mai turned fifteen when Giải Phóng happened. After the war, her father was sent up North to a labor camp for reeducation. His sin: serving in the military in South Vietnam. They sent him there to die along with many officers. Her mother and the young children were loaded up on a truck one day and brought to this *Kinh Tế Mới* near the Cambodian border, a new-economic zone. They cut down trees to clear an acre of land, planted manioc and peanuts, fought the ant hills, scorpions and the red mud to eke out a living. They ate what they could grow on the hard and shallow soil. For years, Mai craved the taste of rice. She used to walk along the canal and dream about how the young rice would taste. That was all she could think about: the taste of rice.

She married a young boy in the same lot. With pale skin, a skinny tall frame and slender fingers, he looked out of place in the scorching heat and muddy fields. It was easy for Mai to fall in love with him. She thought that one day they would both go back to Saigon where he could be a teacher while she raised children. Baby Dan came early, when she was just 17. It was the best thing that had ever happened in that house, where they lived with her mother and her brother. The laughs and cries of the little baby lit up the hut, far brighter than the kerosene lamps.

After the baby died, her husband became silent. He worked, smoked, drank, and then one day he disappeared. Mai had no idea where he went and she never heard from him again. She hoped that he would find a woman to care for him, feed him, and make love to him. She hoped that he had the chance to go back to school and find a teaching job in the city.

●●●

"How is the mango business?" Mai asked her brother when she arrived at the farm.

"Good year!" Hai said. "Really good! People from Saigon came and paid in advance, as soon as the trees flowered. We have the best mango in the country. The heat here is good for mango." He waved his hand at the acres of green mango trees around the farm house. It was February and the trees had already been stripped of all their fruits. There were only a few left here and there.

Hai ran the family farm. Growing up here, he never knew much about school. He didn't get to read books and dream about life in the big city. His hair had turned red from the scorching sun and his skin the same color as the earth around him. He sat with his one leg up, knee touching his chin, the other one folded neatly on the seat. He pulled on the cheap cigarette that was imported from somewhere across the Cambodian border. The smoke drifted slowly out of his mouth, around his stained teeth.

"I have to go visit our mother's grave," Mai said.

She rummaged through her belongings and found the roll of incense sticks she bought on her trip down. The afternoon sun angled now so walking a mile in the heat was bearable. She followed a red dirt road along a small canal running west, along a rubber tree plantation and manioc farms. She reached the cemetery behind the Catholic church. The sun glowed red behind the eucalyptus trees that separated the graves from the manioc fields. The graves were in good repair. The lots were filling up every year.

Even in death, religion mattered: Catholics were buried on one side, Buddhists another.

The incense smoke burned her eyes but she didn't bother to fight back the tears. Mai lit three incense sticks and placed them in front of her mother's grave. She wished that she had been able to bury Dan here so that she could burn incense and pray for his soul every Tết. She had tried to find where they buried the baby on the side of that fifteen-mile stretch of road. The flooded rice paddies had erased all traces of the grave. Years passed searching and she simply gave up trying. She could only hope and pray that his soul would be free of this world.

• • •

The day baby Dan died, it rained and rained. Mai held him like a bundle of firewood. Her husband pressed silently on the bike pedals with her on the back. At the hospital, the doctor declared their baby was dead prior to their arrival. Mai and her husband had no plans for what to do next. They would probably find a dry plot back in the village to bury him but they were so exhausted. They couldn't go on anymore. They were hungry, they had no energy and it rained so hard, so very hard, and the red mud, fifteen miles of red mud to go.

They fell down and couldn't get up. Still more miles to go and they couldn't go even one more minute. It was pitch dark.

"Let's bury him here," her husband said. She was already numb from the cold and the weariness and sadness. She couldn't think. She couldn't move.

He went down to a ditch next to the road and placed the baby down deep. With his hands, he scooped enough dirt to cover up the body and stuck a branch on top.

"Let's come back tomorrow when it's light and we can get some help," he said.

She followed, walking behind him like a shadow of a ghost. One step followed another, and another, like the undead.

The next morning, they gathered brother Hai and a couple of neighbors to go look for the body. They searched the side of the road, they looked for the stick that marked the grave, they searched everywhere. The rain had washed the red mud over everything. Red mud covered the fields, miles and miles of mud. Nothing but red mud.

● ● ●

"Why don't you come back here and live with us? We have money now. You don't have to carry a heavy load every day, getting harassed by cops, treated like nothing by strangers," Hai said.

"Too many bad memories," Mai said.

Hai left it at that. He had asked the same question many times before and the answer had always been the same.

Many things had changed. The family house had been much improved in recent years. The road had been paved and there was electricity throughout the village. The new-economic zone had become what it was promised to be. It only took thirty years to get here—so many broken lives along the way, hers included. The road home had been the burial site of her baby, and her youth. Everywhere she looked, baby Dan may have been there in spirit. His body had become part of the landscape, the rice fields, the steaming heat and the red mud.

The Last Jungle

"Do you know that Uncle Thôi is living here now?" Hòa broke the news.

"Where?" I asked.

"Here in this village, within half a mile," he confirmed. "He usually comes around at dinner time and asks for a beer. He says he is cutting down on the drinking."

Whoa. I was surprised. I heard he had returned to Vietnam to live after several years in Tennessee, but now he had come to live in this village, just like my father before he died.

Uncle Thôi is the second youngest of my father's siblings and only ten years older than me. Thôi literally means "stop or enough" in Vietnamese. My paternal grandparents decided that they had had their last child but one more aunt was born afterwards. She didn't live to adulthood.

He was one of my favorite uncles when I was a kid. He used to treat me to every kind of dessert in Hội An, my father's birthplace. For several days of Tết, I played cards with my uncles and aunts and they spoilt me and my brothers with sweets. Those were the happy days before the war came closer to home, before he became a soldier.

Every six months, he came by to stay a few days with us in Saigon. He carried a green duffle bag and wore only military fatigues without decorations for his ranks. Even though he was our uncle, he never yelled at us for messing around with his deadly machete and bayonet, but he was strict about the Carbine rifle that he hid away. My mother liked him because he never gave her a hard time like the rest of my father's relatives. I heard he had a wife and a son, but I didn't know anything about them. He always had an easy smile and enjoyed the food my mother cooked for him before going back to the jungle.

Short and wiry like a mountain lion, he carried with him a stealthiness as if he could disappear into the trees whenever he stood still. He drank a lot of beer, cognac, whiskey, and farmers' rice wines, but he never smoked. When he wasn't drinking, he roughhoused with us. We squeezed his rock-hard biceps, pounded his rippling stomach and called him Uncle Tarzan. Every afternoon, he lined us up for karate lessons, "Hi-yah! Yell when you punch! Tighten your fist. Harder!"

After the fall of Saigon, like many military personnel of the defeated South Vietnam army, he was sent to a re-education camp for years. I heard he survived eight years of hard labor and came back barely alive. Afterwards, he and his then wife applied for immigrant status and came to join his son in Memphis, Tennessee. We saw each other once in California after his wife left him. "I am thinking of going back to Vietnam to live. There is nothing here for me." He told me.

● ● ●

"Let's go visit him," I got up from the hammock.

"Sure. He will love to see you. It must have been a long time." Hòa slipped into his flip flops.

We walked half a mile toward the village market. In front of a street-front house, Uncle Thôi's now wife ran a stall selling sticky rice. My new aunt-in-law is a lot younger than me, and of course younger than him. She waved at Hòa as we approached.

"Is this your brother from America? Come in. Come in," she shouted in my direction.

I said hello to her and walked in the living room. There he was, Uncle Thôi in the flesh. It had been about two decades since I last saw him in America. He was much shorter than the Tarzan I remembered. Near eighty, he stooped a little but was still strong. His hearing was almost gone—I had to shout in his ear a few times for him to register. Many years with heavy artillery must have blown out his eardrums. His cropped hair was all white and his dentures clacked as he talked.

"You know, Thế has just died. Last month," he meant his son in Tennessee.

"Oh no! He was so young." I was shocked to hear of my cousin's death. "Did you go to his funeral?"

"My previous wife took care of that. I just prayed for him."

"So how did he die?" I prodded.

"Lung cancer. He smoked too much," Uncle Thôi looked at the ceiling for a while. "I never smoked. It was dangerous to light up in the dark jungle when you're on a secret mission. Easy target for snipers."

I looked around the house, on the walls were some acrylic paintings. One depicted the Virgin Mary with Vietnamese facial features. One was a self-portrait of himself in front of my grandmother's house in Hội An, where he grew up. Others were landscapes of different seasons in the United States. He painted with bright colors, unmixed. They radiated cheerfulness, like the rays emanating from the Madonna's face.

"Are these your paintings, Uncle Thôi?" I was really impressed. My tough uncle, a trained killer, could paint.

"When I came to America, I went to a community college and took classes. I still want to paint but I can't find supplies and canvas here. Other people can sing, write poetry, or play music. I love to paint."

My aunt-in-law came in with a few sweets and a pot of tea. She moved around quietly like a servant and went back to tend to the business facing the street. He stood up and poured tea in our cups. The way he stooped to serve with his shaky hands reminded me so much of my father after he came back from re-education camp. They just seemed so much skinnier, slower, and the light had gone out of their eyes in a zombie sort of way. Gone was the martial arts teacher that I used to see in him when he taught us karate. Not the Tarzan who threatened to kick our butts when we touched his forbidden gear.

"What did you do in the war, Uncle Thôi? Where did you serve?" I wanted to hear his stories.

"After years in the tanks division, I joined the special forces to spot targets for the Americans. Usually, my mission was to sneak in, mark the coordinates, and call for the bombers to take them out. One day in Củ Chi where the VC fought from tunnels, I was too close to the enemy and took a hand grenade four meters away. U.S. helicopters rescued me and their surgeons saved my life." He lifted his T-shirt to show me the big scar. It ran vertically from his chest down past the belly button like a dark brown snake.

"Can't you just retire then?" I asked.

"The army didn't let me go. After my injury, they reassigned me to the academy in Thủ Dức to train cadets. And then we lost the war and I went to re-education without any hope of release. The new regime expected me to die."

"Tell me, what happened after Giải Phóng? Where did they send you?" I wondered which prison camp he was banished for re-education. Military men like him usually served life-sentences in the most fearsome mountainous places. They were free labor to clear the remote jungles in to grow crops and prepare for future settlements.

"A jungle in the central highlands, somewhere near the border with Cambodia. I didn't think I would ever get out alive, but one day, they gave me a blanket and a kilo of rice and let me take the train back to Saigon."

"How long were you in labor camp, Uncle Thôi?"

"Long enough for most of us to die. Long enough to make sure you will fear the sight of guns, a whip, or any person in uniform. Most of all, you will fear hunger, malaria, tuberculosis, leeches, and the shivering cold."

I must have opened a faucet, because the stories kept flowing.

"My first wife left me when I was in labor camp. She gave me up for dead and I can't really blame her. I was never good to her even before re-education. I was gone all the time to the frontline. I was never there for her and my son." He stared at the pictures on the wall. "Later, Thế asked me to join him in America, so I came with my second wife."

"Why are you back here again, Uncle Thôi? What's wrong with Tennessee?"

"My second wife left me. I was drinking too much. I had a violent temper. I had nightmares of the battles, the bombs, blown-up bodies, and then the jungle camp. Painting helped calm me down."

"So why Vietnam again? With all the bad memories?" I kept digging.

"It's just too late for old people like me and your father to fit in America. We don't speak the language, can't drive, can't work. What do you do all day long? I was just a burden to my kids, but most of all, I was lonely."

I remember clearly my father's loneliness in a room all day long in America. He finally decided to come back to the farm to live the rest of his days.

"So, I came back to Saigon but it's too noisy and crowded for me. I like it here in the country, a bit hot without air-conditioning, but I can get around. My wife is young and strong so she will take good care of me."

"Please come for dinner with us tonight," Hòa invited him.

"Sure. Just me. She will spend some time with her parents."

●●●

Later in the day, Uncle Thôi came to Hòa's farm for dinner. He rode an electric golf cart around the village, real cool and energy efficient. Besides, he couldn't ride a motorcycle anymore.

Hòa went out to get a six pack of beer, just in case. Uncle Thôi seemed to forget what he said earlier about not drinking anymore.

Under the mango tree, we had a family dinner like old times. He called me by my child hood name: "Con Xê, I am so glad to see you again. It has been too long."

"Uncle Tarzan, to your health." I clinked my beer glass with him. I saw a twinkle in his eyes.

His cell phone rang. He picked up and answered the call. A loud woman's voice came across, something about a house she wanted him to look at. He said something to her about tomorrow and hung up.

"I am looking for a house to buy. I have looked at dozens but nothing worked out. The ones on the main street like this are too expensive. The ones in the back alleys are cheaper but my wife can't do her business," he explained. Unlike America, properties facing the busy streets are most desirable in Vietnam.

Hòa chuckled, "That's the dilemma. I feel sorry for your agent. I don't think you can find anything here, not like in the old days in this new-economic zone."

"They used to be so cheap. I should have bought one years ago."

"What about staying here?" Hòa pressed him. "Your rent is very low, right?"

"But where do we live when the owners decide to sell this house? Besides, I don't know how long I will be around and she needs a place to work."

Then we talked about playing tourist the next morning. Uncle Thôi suggested, "Let's go someplace new. Have you seen the new Bà Đen Mountain? They have constructed a huge statue of Lady Buddha at the top and there are cable gondolas to take you up there."

"Unfortunately, the cable is down," Hòa had already checked.

"How about the Cao Đài Temple? It is a famous tourist attraction in the town of Tây Ninh."

"There is a special prayer event going on. They won't let us in." Hòa had also checked.

"I have an idea," I volunteered. "When I was on the way here, I saw a sign about a national park named Xa Mát. It mentioned wildlife and historical landmarks. I would like to check it out."

I had been back to Vietnam many times and made visits to every national park in the South. None of my ecologist and birder friends had ever mentioned Xa Mát.

"It's not far from here. Maybe twenty kilometers toward the border, a little north of us," Hòa knew this place. "I have lived here all my life but have never been to Xa Mát. Never had any reason to go."

"I have not been there. A park, you say?" Uncle Thôi didn't sound very enthusiastic. He probably preferred someplace with food and drinks.

"So, let's do that. We can go to Xa Mát and be back by lunch. Then I will pack and go to Saigon," I decided. I was excited to see what kind of wildlife this park has to offer, especially in the bird department.

• • •

The next morning, after breakfast at my aunt's food stall, we got ready to go to Xa Mát. Thanh, my driver, was having coffee under the mango tree and chatting with Hòa about the history of the mango farm. He was glad we were going to Xa Mát because he had never been there either. One more place for him to explore and add to his database of experience.

Thanh checked Google Maps quickly for directions. "According to GPS, it is only twenty minutes from here, a little bit north and heading straight to the border with Cambodia."

We loaded up the small SUV with some water and snacks. Uncle Thôi sat up front. My brother Hòa, his daughter Xíu, and I in the back. The road to Xa Mát was the same as everywhere in rural Vietnam. What used to be all green fields were now developed with houses and store fronts along the roadsides. Many people had recently moved here to this frontier area near the Cambodian border.

Then the housing developments stopped and we entered a different world. A rusty sign marked the boundary of the park and an iron liftgate stood open. No guards. No booth. Just a narrow road straight ahead.

"Should we go in?" I asked Thanh.

"Let's look for a guard," Thanh pointed at a house about a hundred meters inside the park.

We drove up. It sure looked like a forest guard house with a flag pole outside. Nobody came out to stop us or to collect fees. Thanh got out of the car and walked to it. He knocked on the door. After a moment, someone opened it without stepping outside. A few minutes later, Thanh came back to the car.

"It's OK to go in. The park is open."

I was glad we didn't come all this way for nothing.

The road ahead of us was narrow and straight, with a power-line running along it. Both sides of the road were a thick jungle we couldn't have walked through. Tall Dipterocarpus and Ficus trees jutted out from the understory of vines and Melaleuca, their branches spread out like big arms. Not much light could reach the jungle floor through that vegetation. The jungle went on for miles without a clearing anywhere. I have seen a few jungles in Vietnam but this one was among the wildest. No forest management had occurred here at all for decades, it seemed.

"This is no park, it's a jungle," Uncle Thôi said from the front seat. "They said it's a *Vườn* Quốc Gia, a national garden, but there is nothing here."

"This is what the new-economic zone used to look like," Hòa exclaimed. "Just like where we came to live after Giải Phóng. For the first year, we lived in the jungle like this while surviving on government rations of barley and cassava. We ate snakes, termites, and everything that crawled. Things got better after the village co-op dug a canal to bring in water so we could grow rice and other crops. When I got tired of doing the same as everyone else, I switched to mango."

I admire Hòa's resilience. I could never do what he did to convert a jungle to a successful mango farm with his own hands. He was still a young boy when my family was banished to this jungle as punishment for my father serving as a military officer in the South. Just the mention of the words "new-economic zone" could scare the daylight out of city folks like us, Vietnamese urbanites who have never lived with nature. I grew up with horror stories of jungles as dangerous places with man-eating tigers and poisonous snakes. Only the tribal folks lived in the jungles and practiced shifting cultivation. Unfortunately for them, their territory is quickly disappearing, taken by people from the lowlands for coffee and tea plantations.

I had never appreciated the beauty and value of the jungles until I became a forester and realized there was not much of this natural resource left after the destruction of war, followed by deforestation for timber and housing development in the aftermath.

I looked for any billboard to indicate a tourist attraction and found only one. Across from a small dirt parking lot an obscure sign read, *Trail to historical landmarks. Guided tour only.*

"Historical landmarks mean bomb craters and tunnels. You don't want to wander off the trail. There might still be unexploded ordnance," Hòa said. "We found craters and bombs when we first got here too. A few people got their hands and feet blown off by cluster bomblets."

"Sheesh!" I mumbled to myself.

A few further miles, we came upon a military base. A guard in uniform with an AK-47 dangling across his chest stood in front of the gate to an imposing building.

"Let's ask for directions," Thanh got out of the car. I truly admired his courage to talk to strangers. I hated encountering people with guns, especially in remote places.

They chatted in a friendly fashion while the guard pointed his finger towards the west. Thanh nodded his thanks and climbed back in the driver's seat.

"The border is only another kilometer or so. Then we make a right turn and come out the main entrance of the park. We happen to have come in through the back door."

A few minutes later, we reached Cambodia. Beyond the iron liftgate, the border police stood guard with AK-47's. We turned right as instructed and went north. A small dry creek demarcated the border between the two neighboring countries. The vegetation was the same on both sides.

"This whole area was the war zone between us and the Khmer, for centuries. After Giải Phóng, we invaded them and they pushed us back. Now there is a clear border. You can also see why there is a military base on this side, just in case," Hòa explained to me.

"But why is this a park now?" I had one last question.

"Who knows. The Government makes decisions on all lands. Maybe they don't know what to do with it yet. Maybe they wait for the tourists to come, but tourists go to beaches and island resorts. Who wants to see this jungle full of bomb craters and tunnels? Maybe they will sell off the land when people run out of places to live. Maybe soon."

Ahead of us, I saw many signs of birdlife on this deserted road along the creek. A large blue and black bird flew past. I asked

Thanh to stop the car and got out with my camera and the long lens to get a few shots of some endemic birds here.

Everyone got off to stretch their legs but Uncle Thôi stayed in the car, his eyes closed. He might have been taking a nap.

I walked ahead with Xíu as she pointed out the blue-and-white Flycatchers playing hide and seek along the creek. A flock of Yellow-vented Bulbuls flew by. I never got a good look at the large bird again but got a few good shots of the Common Iora, a tiny yellow bird with steely grey eyes.

Hòa walked along at a distance, smoking a cigarette, without any interest in the wildlife. He must have thought I had gone mad.

I enjoyed birding so much I forgot about Uncle Thôi. By the time we got back in the car, it must have been near noon and soon we must go back to the farm and then I would say goodbye and head back to Saigon.

"Please leave already. There is nothing to see here," Uncle Thôi moaned when we jumped in.

"Are you bored? Are you tired?" I was wondering if he'd spent too much time in the hot car.

"It is a jungle. Just another jungle," he closed his eyes and shook his head. His forehead was all sweaty.

"Do you need some water, Uncle Thôi?" I thought he was dehydrated.

"I fought in a jungle like this in Củ Chi, full of tunnels and booby traps. They almost killed me. Then I went to a re-education camp, a prison like this place. I almost died there too from Malaria and dysentery. I have seen enough here." Uncle Tarzan couldn't take much more of this jungle.

I realized it was like torture to him, all over again. I had no idea what it was like for him to spend days and nights in a dark jungle for years not knowing whether or not he would ever see his family again. I could not imagine how my brother managed to scratch out a living in the new-economic zone in a place like this. For me, Xa Mát could be a birders' paradise but for them, they were reliving the nightmares they must have wanted to forget.

Part of me wants this jungle to remain this way for as long as possible. After all, it may be the only place in this country that hasn't been destroyed and developed into a resort and theme park, or for growing crops. Maybe it is best that the détente with Cambodia will keep it safe from the chain saws, roadbuilding, and housing development, but I know it is only a matter of time before it will be full of people who need land to make a living.

We left Xa Mát the way we came in. There were no signs, no guards, no fees. It's just a jungle that time forgot, for now.

A Place to Land

When I saw Tràm Chim Park in 1994 on my first trip back to Vietnam, my heart was still raw from the reentry. The country was beginning to recover from a devastating bloody war and another two decades of a crushing economic embargo that the U.S. led against an old enemy. With that wide open heart, I came to this desolate place in Đồng Tháp, the poorest and most remote province in Vietnam. I traveled with friends on a mission for the International Crane Foundation to help restore the habitat for the Eastern Sarus Crane.

Dr. Kiet welcomed us at the guest house. About twenty years my senior, the botany professor had undergone the most rigorous training in France and become the resident expert in all living plants in Vietnam. He had collaborated with the International Crane Foundation with the restoration effort from the very beginning.

He shook my hand with both of his. "I understand you are a forester."

"I work for the Research branch in the U.S. Forest Service. I am more of a manager now. My knowledge is a mile wide and one inch deep."

He explained the history of the park's name. "People remembered that long ago, the Melaleuca (Tràm) forest and the surrounding wetlands had been the winter home for the birds (Chim) and named the place Tràm Chim. During the war, the Melaleuca forests were defoliated and burned to the ground. It took twenty years of peace for the land to start healing and the vegetation to come back. So did the Eastern Sarus Crane. The conservation community around the world jumped at the chance to save the threatened species and pledged to help establish a permanent reserve for them here. Well, you will find this interesting since you know about trees. You see the Melaleuca? It is the only native Melaleuca species in Vietnam."

"I thought all Melaleuca came from Australia. How did it get here?" I asked.

"*Melaleuca cajuputi* has been here at least for centuries. Our fossil records of seeds and pollen showed that. The forest is an important reason for the cranes to return and it must be protected."

I asked Dr. Kiet why he was worried about these small trees.

He said, "People use the leaves to make essential oil. They also need the small-diameter timber for charcoal and makeshift homes but more is shipped to the cities to be used as underground enforcement for buildings. If we let them be exploited, the forest will be all gone."

Indeed, I had seen boatloads of skinny Melaleuca stems heading toward Saigon. There was always a big demand for them in the construction business.

"Here, the cranes need this forest for proper ecological functioning of their habitat, basically to maintain the natural hydrologic cycles of the wetland. The challenge now is to work with the farmers to protect the park, but it's not going to be easy because they want to take and clear the land to grow crops."

In the buffer zone around the park, villagers were still set-tling in. Landless people from all over came to settle in the buffer zone around the park. They tried to make a living farming the soil that had turned acidic after years of burning and was still toxic with Agent Orange residues. They built their homes with small Melaleuca timber and roofed them with coconut palm fronds. Outdoor toilets and monkey bridges hung perilously over the canals, choked with water hyacinth. All the roads were still unpaved. Only a few houses near the main roads had just begun to get electricity and most were still lit with kerosene lamps at night.

Every afternoon after a long day of surveying the park, Dr. Kiet and I stood on the observation deck of the three-story govern-ment building to watch the cranes feeding in the field. Hundreds of them dotted the sky and landed on the plain of reeds in the set-ting sun. Not long after that trip, Dr. Kiet retired and handed the mission to his protégé who became a life-long friend to me.

• • •

Ten years after I met Dr. Kiet, I began working closely with Triet, one of Dr. Kiet's finest students. I first met Triet in 1997 when he was finishing his PhD program at the University of Wisconsin in Madison while working for the International Crane Foundation (ICF). Right after his graduation, Triet returned to Vietnam and played a key role as the facilitator of a conference along with Jeb, senior ecologist of ICF and Triet's mentor.

The conference convened by The Đồng Tháp provincial gov-ernment in 1999 was perhaps the most pivotal moment in the history of Tram Chim Park. After it was officially established and recognized by the government of Vietnam as a national park, the province needed a management plan to balance the ecological, social, and economic needs of the area to ensure its sustainability.

I was invited to the conference along with a few colleagues to provide technical assistance. John, forest supervisor, and Kathy, wetland ecologist, and I were the U.S. Forest Service team.

"You and Triet are the only ones here who understand everything, both in Vietnamese and English," John said.

"It's not what is said. You have to listen to what they mean. The Vietnamese are not always direct. If they don't say anything, it means No. If they say let's decide tomorrow, it also means No." I warned John that the nuances would be lost in translation.

The province leader was an older gentleman, Bac Ba, who loved the crane. He grew up fighting against the South Vietnamese and American armies and now he was in position to make decisions about a place he loved.

Bac Ba opened the meeting with a short speech, "We are here to develop a plan on how to manage 7,000 hectares of land we have set aside. We have the scientific community with one voice, the farmers with another, and they are not the same. We need to address the issues so we can have cranes, timber, rice, and fish, and avoid conflicts between the farmers and the park. The problems are not easy to solve, but together, let's work out a plan."

The local representatives spoke first. I translated for our team. Just the essence of what they said.

"We are poor farmers. This province is the only place we can call home. We have nowhere else to go so we end up here. We need land to grow rice, water for fish, timber and firewood, and food to feed our families. The poor acidic soil can only yield one rice crop a year. If we don't have access to the park, we are going to starve."

Then Jeb spoke. He had been working at Tràm Chim for at least a decade and was passionate about saving the cranes. A stoic Norwegian from Wisconsin, he came straight to the point:

"The cranes need a healthy ecosystem to provide them food and shelter for six months between December and April. I see two issues here. Number One, the water level has been kept too high and we need a drawdown during the dry season. If not, the vegetation will rot and not provide the tubers the cranes eat. Number Two, the park has to be kept as an integral ecosystem. It is not big enough as it is, and if fragmented it will no longer function properly."

"Why can't we divide this land into sections," the farmers countered. "One for fish, one for timber, one for the birds?"

"Fragmentation of the park will spell death for the birds," Jeb replied bluntly. We can manage some extraction and use, only some, but I am totally against dividing the park into pieces. Plus, we need to manage the water levels so that there are seasonal changes. A wetland is not always wet. Sometimes it needs to be dry, and even to burn now and then."

The mention of fire ignited the hot dry heap of fuels in the room. It's the dreaded topic. The last fire during a recent drawdown had burned down parts of the Melaleuca forest and cost the park managers and village leaders their jobs. That's why the water level had been kept high since.

"We can manage fire," Jeb continued. "We have the expertise to do controlled burns and suppress fire to keep the village safe."

"That's easy for you to say since you are from America. We don't have resources to do that," said the opposition.

"We have some fire experts here, and we will send for help to develop a fire management plan," Jeb insisted, looking at the Forest Service delegation. John nodded agreement since he had real fire management experience of a national forest in California.

The meeting went on for hours about the topics of fire, sectioning the park, and water level management. It was an impasse when we adjourned at the end of the day.

The next day Bac Ba informed us during a luncheon that he would invite a U.S. expert from the Forest Service to help with a fire management plan for the park. I said that I would make it happen. He said nothing further about the water level or the sectioning issues.

After the conference, we had a free day for field trips. Jeb, Kathy, Triet, and a few other ecologists went to the Melaleuca forest to survey and monitor biodiversity in the park. John and I went to the village to drink tea and talk with the farmers.

While I was just about to enjoy the second frozen yogurt, a man came rushing into our roadside restaurant, got off his bike and yelled:

"They were bit! They were bit!"

It took a little more of his explaining before we figured out that the ecologists walked into a hornet's nest and were swarmed. Triet along with an English and a Cambodian scientist were in serious trouble. Kathy got away safely when she dove into the canal. Jeb got a few bites but was too stoic to show any pain. The three victims were carried to the only nursing facility in the village for triage and first aid treatments. We quickly rushed there to see them.

"Oh! My God! The pain!" Triet was stung at least fifty times with welts over his head and arms. So were the other two.

There was nothing the so-called hospital in the village could do for them. They didn't even have the medications needed for bee stings. It was decided to move them to Cao Lanh, the seat of the province government fifteen kilometers away. I boarded the old Toyota van with the three patients and headed there. The road to Cao Lanh was still under construction and full of big rocks. We drove slowly over the rough road and every time the van hit a pothole, the moans got loud. Then the van stopped.

The left rear tire blew out as we were half-way to Cao Lanh. Lucky for us, there was a usable spare tire. I found the tire iron and went to work in the midday sun and got the job done. "I hope we don't get another flat tire," I mumbled to myself.

Triet and the others were in the Cao Lanh hospital for three days. They got the royal treatment because Bac Ba made sure of it: IV drips, pain medications, and even an ultrasound.

"The good news is you don't have twins," I humored Triet when he was awake.

"Thank you for staying with me," Triet grimaced. He managed a joke. "The Viet Cong had stopped fighting but the bees didn't get the message that war was over twenty years ago."

I counted my blessings. If I or any of my American colleagues were bit, or God forbid, died, I could have spent the rest of my career filing reports and paperwork to explain why we violated every safety precaution in the Forest Service Manual.

Even after that near-death experience, Triet continued to return to Tram Chim Park and took over the ecologist role that Jeb had played for a decade. As a regional expert for ICF, he traveled throughout Southeast Asia to work with nature reserves in Cambodia and Myanmar to expand the habitats for the Sarus Crane. Every now and then, I asked him about new developments at Tràm Chim.

Triet assured me, "We are protecting the park from poaching and timber theft. We have a good park director and a hundred staff members taking care of business."

"What about the crane counts?" I asked.

"Not as many as before. This year, only a few dozen. The park management still kept the water level too high in fear of fire. Even with the fire management plan that your Forest Service expert provided, nobody dared to take risks to implement it."

That was his answer every time I asked about the bird count and the main reason why the cranes had not returned in large numbers. The threat to their winter home was no longer the bombing, burning, and defoliation of the forest. It was now the competition with people and their needs for farming and fishing.

● ● ●

Like most ecologists, Triet is also a birder. He introduced me to myriad species of birds and the equipment for birding. It didn't take much for me to fall in love with this newfound hobby that requires patience, a sharp eye, and a large body of scientific knowledge.

I have counted more than 40 species of birds in my neighborhood in the East Bay of San Francisco. Over two years, I have documented the arrivals and departures of the Bluebirds and Warblers. The rest of the year, I can count on the constant presence of Sparrows, Mockingbirds, and Scrub Jays. When birding action dies down in the neighborhood, I can count on shorebirds at local regional parks. My neighbors always ask, "Where is your camera?" even when they found me weeding in the yard. Before they knew I was not a neighborhood stalker, I had a few confrontations with a couple of folks when they found me on their properties pointing the big lens at their windows.

"Can I help you?" one lady asked. I pointed at the Hummingbird in her yard.

A guy saw me looking up at his roof. "What are you shooting?" I showed him pictures of the Bluebirds on the camera display and he left me alone.

I've gotten to know all the neighbors walking their dogs in the morning, the same time I run my transect. Some have pledged they would vote for me if I ran for Mayor.

• • •

Ten years ago, when I asked Triet for a recommendation of a tour guide to take me and some friends around the Mekong Delta, he said, "You will be happy with Bao. He is my student, a bird expert and adventurer. He is an entrepreneur and is building a small eco-tourism business. He will take care of you."

Bao spent a week guiding us through the Delta. We went south, crossed the two forks of the Mekong River by ferries to the coastal mangrove forests of Cà Mau, the very southernmost tip of the country, and back up along the gulf of Thailand. We stopped wherever we wished to eat and sleep, and toured many nature areas along the way. When not shooting the Herons and Kingfishers, he cradled the big lens like his baby and fell asleep in the boat with it in his lap. Since that trip, we had seen each other a couple more times and I knew his business was booming through Facebook posts.

On my most recent trip in 2023, I asked Bao if I could spend a couple of days at Tràm Chim Park with him. He cheerfully picked me up we drove to Tràm Chim in his small SUV. Thirty years after my first visit with Dr. Kiet, the roads to the park were now all paved, well-lit and decorated with neon lights in the shape of Sarus Crane along the sides. I hardly recognized the landscape that used to be a dusty village, dirt roads and straw huts.

"Welcome to my hotel," Bao announced as we pulled in front of the brightly lit white building with the Wildtour Hotel sign. Something was familiar about this place. On the left of the main building was the annex that used to house the Sarus Crane exhibits. On the right was the courtyard with the volleyball nets and beyond that were the workers' apartments.

"This is the old government guest house!" I recognized the building layout and its strategic location overlooking the park. "It used to be grimy, full of mosquitoes, geckos, and cockroaches."

"Yep! It is. It is a dream come true for me."

"How did you get it? What happened to the park director Hùng?"

"Hùng retired a few years ago. The new director hardly spends time here in the park. The building was empty for a while so I bought it."

"Welcome to Tràm Chim, Anh Hao," Nguyet, Bao's charming wife, greeted me from behind the counter.

In the car before we reached the hotel, Bao had already phoned the kitchen staff to prepare a few dishes for a late dinner. We were the only diners in the big outdoor restaurant in the back of the hotel. It was wonderfully quiet with only sounds of frogs and the nice breeze blowing through the open and spacious dining area covered by a thatched roof with no surrounding walls. On stilts, the dining area rose a few feet above a large fish pond, connected to a canal leading to the wetland park.

They served us a roast duck, stuffed snails, shredded papaya salad, a boiling hot pot and tossed noodles. Bao opened a bottle of local wine made from wild figs.

"Cheers! To your success!" I toasted Bao and Nguyet.

"Everything here is built with local timber and recycled wood. You see, the flooring is rough sawn eucalyptus. The railings are the wood stakes people used for the pepper vines to climb. Over time, what's left of them is the core heartwood. Very rot resistant." He sounded like an architect from an environmental school. In fact, he was pursuing a PhD program in Ornithology and Ecology and had put his education to work.

Indeed, he and Nguyet started a small ecotourism company and with their business savvy, they had built an international network. They cater to small groups of birders (mostly) with trips through Southeast Asia, an unforgettable travel experience that one can't get with other tourism companies that have glossy brochures and spectacular websites about new beach resorts.

"By the way," I announced, "I am a birder now. I have Dr. Triet, your teacher, to thank for that."

"You have fallen into the lime pit," Bao laughed out loud. "There is no escape once you have fallen in."

Bao gave me the same room I had stayed in before but now it was clean and air-conditioned. The bathroom was modern with white a bathtub and tiled floor. All the light switches could be controlled from the bedside. High speed Wi-Fi and internet, of course.

"While you are here, you are my guest." He insisted that I would not have to worry about paying. "I never take money from friends."

"Me, neither," we already knew each other well.

"Tomorrow, we will get up early and go to the park by boat. Six o'clock? I will have coffee ready."

"Yes, six o'clock." I couldn't believe that I had become a genuine birder.

A boatman had been waiting for us at the loading dock of the canal. It was a larger boat hauled by a smaller boat with a motor. It was like a moving living room with enough space for a dinner party of eight people and stable enough to set up tripods for cameras and scopes.

"You need this app," Bao helped me load the Wildtour app to my iPhone. "You can ID the birds by sight and sound too."

We pulled slowly in the larger canal system surrounding the park. In front of me was a large lake, deep and wide even in the dry month of December. Another tourist boat full of birders was not far behind us.

"I don't remember the water level being this high. Aren't we supposed to see more ground and trees?" I asked Bao.

"It is very high, Anh Hao. The management keeps the water level this high all year around," Bao poured me a cup of coffee from his thermos. "It has been good for many bird species, as you can see."

The sun was rising on the quiet water, casting a golden glow on the white and purple water lilies. Along the shore, the Pond Herons stood up to watch us and took off in a white cloud when we got too close. Bronze-winged Jacanas browsed on the lotus patch, walking on the floating leaves with their long spindly toes. Deeper in the reeds, Purple Swamp Hens looked like blue chickens with red caps, hunting for grasshoppers, unperturbed by our engine noise. Further in, a flock of Storks took over a wet meadow digging for snails. Some engaged in an aerial battle over a fresh catch.

Clouds of Swallows followed us as the boat stirred up aquatic insects into the air. Some buzzed right by my nose. I shot away at whatever I could while Bao watched and told me their names. I looked across the horizon for any sign of the cranes, but there was none. Maybe they have not returned yet, I told myself.

Along the way, I saw a couple of fishermen with long poles casting plugs. I asked Bao if they were allowed. He said the park sells permits for fishing. They go after *Cá Lóc*, big snakehead fish.

The sun rose high and as lighting got too harsh for good photography, we headed back to the hotel restaurant.

After another wonderful day with Bao and his charming wife, they took me to the edge of the canal overlooking the park to watch the sunset.

"You have done a great job," I congratulated Bao. "You and your wife. I am happy for you."

"The economy here is much improved. The rice farmers did well. We have many tourists now to support the restaurants and the boat drivers. Tràm Chim is on the map, internationally even." He handed me a cold beer.

As Nguyet took pictures of the Ibis flock against the reddening sky, I asked Bao the inevitable question, "How about the Sarus Crane? Did you see many last season?"

"Sadly, no. They have not returned at all. I don't know where they go but there were less and less returns and last year, there was none."

Postscript: According to Dr. Triet, a reintroduction campaign for the Sarus Crane had begun at the end of 2023 with water drawdown and prescribed fires. Four cranes did return in March 2024. I am hoping that someday soon, the sky will be filled with these magnificent birds and they will land on their ancestral home in the Mekong Delta again.

Gia Định Quán

"I am one of the most successful Vietnamese in America," my friend Tai said. I'd heard this line many times and, like before, I let him talk. "People respect me for my success in business. I have built three companies and sold them for millions." He went on to talk about his house in Atherton, California, set on a ten-acre lot with tall redwoods and old-growth live oaks. When I visited him years ago, he was in the middle of constructing a twelve-bedroom mansion but the project was halted following the real-estate debacle of 2008. I guessed his Disneyland castle was completed now.

After many long years, Tai and I had met again, this time at a fancy restaurant in Saigon. He was on a business trip and I was here to explore the Mekong Delta with other friends.

"Come see me in Atherton," Tai continued once he returned from a trip to the toilet to recycle some beer. "Atherton has the highest number of billionaires per capita in the U.S." That was another one of Tai's favorite lines.

For the next half hour, Tai ranted about his real estate ventures and the fortune he's amassed over the years. "Americans look down on foreigners because they have to pay taxes to support them," he insisted. "But they look up to people who make more money than they do."

I shook my head in disbelief, "Really? Nobody asks me how much money I make or what I do before they tell me to go back to my country."

Tai couldn't argue with that. He softened. "I mean, generally speaking."

"When you come to Atherton, I will show you my wine collection," Tai changed the subject. "My cave holds hundreds of bottles from France and California."

"Of course, I will make sure to call you," I replied, not sure if I would.

"How is Binh? Have you seen him lately?" Tai finally asked.

"I will see him tomorrow. He is almost totally blind now. That's why he decided to come back and live full-time here in Vietnam so he can get the help he needs to get around. He teaches classical guitar and music composition at a private music school. He told me about a school reunion in a couple of weeks at Gia Định Quán. We are invited."

"I wonder if we will run into any of our old friends," asked Tai.

"Dunno. We were scattered to the winds after Giải Phóng," I said. "It will be nice though to see our favorite hangout again and sit there for a while to remember them."

• • •

Gia Định Quán was the gathering place for those of us who went to Hồ Ngọc Cẩn High School. Just one block away from our school, the garden café rested below large trees and surrounded by fragrant jasmine bushes. It was a cool oasis where we spent hours with a drip coffee and a shared cigarette with the sad anti-war music of Trịnh Công Sơn in the background. We even held our graduation party there. Sometimes when Tai had money, he would treat me to a bowl of Phở. Binh and I often shared a Bánh Mì sandwich stuffed with thin slices of fatty pork, cilantro, and pickled carrots and radish. Mostly, we just went there because there was nowhere else to go.

Tai, Binh and I were classmates for seven years before I left for Australia in 1973. The all-boy public school in Gia Dinh in the suburbs of Saigon was free but its academic performance could compete with any in the country. For seven years, we grew up like brothers. Other than Tai and Binh, I had half a dozen good friends. Occasionally, I got news of one who escaped to America. Most of my friends who stayed back had disappeared from my memory because it had been too long since I saw them last. Some of them I will never forget but I know I have lost them forever. They still haunt me.

I was only thirteen years old when I became aware of sexual orientations among my classmates. Hồng was a very nice boy with a soft voice and artistic talents. He made beautiful greeting cards and embroidered handkerchiefs and often showered me with gifts. A birthday card to me said: "You are my best friend, forever." I don't remember giving him anything back. I was more into roughhousing with other buddies like Binh and Tai. We took up Judo and Karate and practiced martial arts in the school yard every day after class. One time, Hồng came up to me with something in his hand to give to me and before I knew it, I swung around with a roundhouse kick, the technique I had just mastered. I expected him to duck but he didn't and my foot caught him in the chest. He cried and I didn't know what to say to stop his tears. He avoided me after that incident. I have no idea where he is now.

A few others died. Only eighteen years old, Khanh was drafted, sent to boot camp, and then to battlefields in the Central

Highlands. He took a bullet in the stomach while taking a leak in the dark jungle. There was no telling where the shot came from. I heard the bad news when I was a new student in Australia and I sent his mother twenty dollars for his funeral. That's all I could do for him from afar. The only evidence I have of his existence is a B&W photograph of a boy in uniform and a steel helmet, smiling at the sky.

Tai and Binh were my closest boyhood friends, but the two of them could not be more different. Tai was ambitious and driven to achieve wealth and fame; Binh didn't give a shit about money. If there was a role model for irresponsibility, Binh was the best.

While Tai can talk excessively about making money, Binh loves to pontificate about classical music and audio equipment. He has always been critical of my deaf ears: "Listening to digital music is like eating *Phở* without *Nước Mắm*. What you hear is just the part of the music that you sample and not the whole thing. If your ear is any good, you should listen to the analog sounds of vinyl records and 8-tracks. Their sound is high fidelity."

"What about the hissing and the scratching?" I countered the first time he talked with me about Hi-Fi. He looked at me disdainfully. No response followed.

"Music is about sound. Literature is about words," he added, making clear to me another one of his pet peeves. "When you mix words with sound, it's like making an ox carry the extra burden. It's cheating."

It has been his opinion that all the Vietnamese songs we knew and loved with passionate lyrics were a perverted mixed media, a lower art form for the common folk who couldn't appreciate the beauty of instrumental music alone. I am no purist. I still love the sentimental Vietnamese songs that I memorized as a kid, and their words make my heart ache.

One day, I happened to watch a young woman perform on the TV show American Idol. As she raised her voice to sing the classic Spanish bolero "Historia De Un Amor," I fell totally in love with the song. It was not for the lyrics because I didn't understand Spanish very well. It was her hesitant voice and the rhythmic beats of the guitar and the drums that got me. It was not highfalutin stuff, just a human voice harmonized with simple instruments to create the music of the soul. Binh is still right— music is about sound. But the human voice is a beautiful musical instrument, whether you care for the words or not.

Tai, on the other hand, had no use for music. When Saigon fell in 1975, he was picked up by the U.S. Navy and taken to a refugee camp in Guam. Once sponsored by a church to come to the mainland, he found himself alone in a new world, but, like an entrepreneurial seed planted in fertile, capitalistic soil, he germinated and grew. Within a few years, he earned a degree in computer science at a State University and was ready to make money. He was in the right place at the right time. The tech business boomed for Vietnamese immigrants who chose this field in the 1970s and 80s. He began his career with IBM and later established his own tech startups in Silicon Valley.

Tai made a ton of money by outsourcing and offshoring IT work. With the salary of a single computer engineer or a programmer in America, he could hire many equivalent workers in Saigon, where there was a steady supply of well-educated graduates. Every few years, I would get an email from him with a new signature—the new CEO of his latest company.

Despite his bravado and self-promoting bullshit, Binh was entertaining. Unlike Tai, if Binh bragged about something, it was never about money, real estate, or his kids. It was about his new student compositions or the big loudspeakers that he just built for his rich Vietnamese clients. Most of all, he was proud of being authentic to himself despite his many wives' failed attempts to shape him.

Binh elaborated on his failed marriages. "I always tell them up front, I am the way I am. That way they can't blame me afterwards." And when they ultimately divorced, he never fought for his half. He just walked away, which was easy to do because he owned literally nothing. He always somehow ended up with another girlfriend right away, and if she was unlucky enough, he would marry her too.

Compared to Binh and Tai, I was only known for being a reliable academic and public servant. After many long years at UC Berkeley and many degrees, I landed an offer as a scientist for the Forest Service and worked my way steadily up the ladder. I eventually achieved the Senior Executive Service level, the highest rung in the federal government. At the peak of my career, I supervised a few dozen Research Leaders and indirectly led about 200 Ph.D. scientists. My regular paycheck didn't make me rich but, with my frugal lifestyle, I wouldn't have to worry about money anymore.

● ● ●

After the dinner with Tai, I texted Binh: *Tell me where to find you.*

Meet me at the Bach Music School tomorrow, he replied, giving me the coordinates.

I took a taxi to meet him at 5:00 pm, when he was supposed to be finished teaching. The private school in a quiet neighborhood was well lit, clean, and among other new, tall buildings. A young woman was sitting at the school's reception desk browsing the internet on her iPhone.

"I am here to meet Mr. Binh," I announced, using my manager voice. I wanted to impress her as an important friend of the great music teacher.

"Please take a seat. He will be done in a few minutes," she said, barely looking up.

I sat down on a bench across from her, scanning the music books lining the shelves and various instruments hanging on the walls. She continued to scroll on her phone.

A few minutes later, an older student came down the stairs and Binh was right behind him with his hand on the helper's shoulder.

Binh hadn't changed much. He still carried the same strong frame but with more roundness around the waist and long gray hair tied back with an elastic band. We hugged a little longer than socially acceptable, a tight embrace between old friends.

Then he introduced the guy who was helping him down the stairs, "This is Thach, he is here to learn about audio equipment."

Binh handed Thach a wad of cash. Thach counted out the Vietnam *Đồngs* as Binh gave instructions, "How about some roasted chicken, pork sausage, and baguettes. There should be enough there." With that, Binh sent Thach to fetch some food while he and I headed to his apartment.

He put his hand on my shoulder and told me to lead him across the street into a winding alley and, after a few turns, we reached the end of the labyrinth.

"My apartment is on the top floor. We can eat and drink on the rooftop," he said, gesturing to the steep stairs. We climbed all the way to the top of the four-story building with me leading the way.

"Sit here while I find the XO." He disappeared into his little room off the terrace and came back to the rooftop garden with a big bottle of amber cognac that was still bubble-wrapped. "Just the very best for you, man."

The sun had already set and lights went up all over the city. A few mosquitoes found my ankles. Thach, Binh's loyal helper, came back with the food and spread it out on the round concrete picnic table. He broke up some ice and the three of us drank the XO.

Binh spoke to Thach between bites of chicken, "You know that Hao and I have been friends for more than fifty years? Since when we were little kids."

"That's amazing," Thach said. "That's as long as I have been alive."

"He was a good student and got a scholarship to go to Australia. I went abroad too, but to fight in Cambodia." Binh cracked a crooked smile.

I asked Binh about his years after Giải Phóng, "Why Cambodia? Didn't we have enough death and dying in Vietnam?" I never understood why North Vietnam invaded its neighbor so soon after conquering the South.

"The Vietnamese war with Cambodia was inevitable. There were always border conflicts with them." Binh lit a cigarette and took a long drag. "So, Premier Le Duan wanted to take Cambodia and annex it."

"I see," I said. "The North was already on a roll after the fall of Saigon. Just one more push and we would be formidable in Southeast Asia."

"We could have won easily. Problem is China wouldn't let it happen and backed the Khmer Rouge to stop us. After ten years of fighting, we had to pull back. Just like America's defeat, we gave up."

Binh turned to look at me and changed subjects, "We made a promise to meet again in ten years in front of our school, remember?"

"I am sorry I couldn't come back." I had never forgotten the promise we made to each other the day I left Saigon back in 1973. But when the time came ten years later, I was still a new immigrant in America and couldn't return. Refugees were still leaving Vietnam by boats and the exiles like me were not allowed back. We focused on starting new lives and helping the people we left behind.

"I knew you couldn't, but I was there the whole day. Just to think of us." His words brought tears to my eyes.

Binh poured me another shot of the XO, "I didn't know how to find you. I asked your mother and she said you went to America. I thought I would never see you again."

I said, "And I thought you were dead since nobody knew where you were after you went to Cambodia."

"Thanks to Tai, I found out where you were when I got out to America. He gave me your phone number." He reached out to grab my shoulder. "Drink up, my friend. Let's not lose each other again."

Binh suddenly remembered something. "Hang on, I need to make a call." He brought his iPhone up to his nose and found the large number to dial.

"*I am free tomorrow night. Just come to my place after six,*" he said as he lowered his voice an octave. The female voice on the phone said yes. Binh put down the phone and turned to me with a big grin.

"Was it your wife?" I asked.

"No, she is out of town, working in Dalat," he said without further explanation.

It was getting late but before we parted ways, Binh asked me to take a trip with him to Bến Tre, a town nearby, so we could spend a few days on the road together.

"Just like when we were kids. You, me and Tai. We loved our bike trips even though we couldn't go far and didn't have money." It sure was tempting but I had already booked other trips.

Binh tried again to convince me, "We are also getting old. There won't be much time for us to be together like this again. I can take you to all the local attractions along the way. Bến Tre has a lot of playhouses. Some are luxury, some are downright cheap. You need to live a little."

I knew what he meant. He was trying to tempt me with women, his favorite form of entertainment. His obsession had gotten me in trouble many times when we were kids.

"No, man," I declined. "I have too many other things on my itinerary. My time is all spoken for." Reluctantly, he let it drop but still promised to find me a girlfriend.

"I may not be rich," Binh said, "but I am the master in the art of living."

● ● ●

The day came for the reunion with our high school friends. I arrived at the cross section where the garden restaurant used to be as the sun was setting. I looked for the big trees that shaded the courtyard but there were none. I headed to the street corner hoisting a neon sign with the restaurant name. A man in a green Grab taxi vest sat on his bike smoking a cigarette when I approached.

"Is this Gia Định Quán?" I asked.

He nodded, "This is what's left of it."

I asked him what happened and he told me the owner sold away most of the land for a lot of money. Gia Định Quán is now a plain street corner restaurant with an air-conditioned dining room and a few tables outside.

I found Binh waiting inside the restaurant. He had booked the private room and already ordered food and beer.

"I have invited all the Hồ Ngọc Cẩn alumni that I know. Probably two dozen guys."

Our old classmates slowly arrived and Tai was in the mix. The young boys that I went to school with had turned to wrinkled old men. Binh knew them all because he had been living in Saigon for a while, but I couldn't tell who was who.

"Remember Thuy? He used to be our class president?" Binh was trying to help me.

Thuy remembered me. "Are you Hao, the quiet student who never said anything?"

"You have a good memory. I am sorry I don't recognize anybody. I have been away too long. Fifty years since I graduated and left the country." I confessed.

"It has been a whole lifetime," Thuy said. And we didn't find anything more to say.

After a lot of hellos and re-introductions, I sat down around the long table with two dozen old men in the air-conditioned room. A young woman came in with plates of boiled chicken, pork sausages, shredded cabbage salad and a boiling hot pot of rice porridge. Then she carted in boxes of Heineken beer and passed cans around. It didn't take much time before the first round of beer was consumed and everyone started shouting the most famous Vietnamese chant: *Một Hai Ba Dzô*, One Two Three, Drink!

The oldest alumnus, sitting at the head of the table, obviously the ringleader, stood up to kick off the formal part of the event. He listed off the names of school friends and teachers who had recently passed away. Then he made a toast to those of us who had managed to survive and come back from afar.

With more rounds of beer, and cigarettes, the group grew louder and friendlier. Tai was doing his best to impress them with his success stories. Binh was sharing stories about his musical triumphs and sexual conquests. I couldn't think of anything to say to connect with them, nothing at all.

I looked around the table at the men eating boiled chicken and getting drunk. They lived there, in the squalor of Saigon's alleys. For many of them, they had never left the country or breathed clean air. They had never had the true freedom to say whatever they believed in. Many of them had never experienced solitude and enjoyed it. I would have been just like them had I never left.

It got late but the locals wanted to keep partying. They turned on the Karaoke machine and prepared for a long night of singing and drinking. Binh was ready to bow out because he detested the bad music. Tai and I were also looking for a graceful exit. We shared the cost of the dinner since we were the rich men from America. It was also expected of us.

Near midnight, the three of us stood alone on the sidewalk. Binh and Tai had planned to go to Bến Tre together for a couple of days. "I expect a full report," I told them.

"Even if I die tomorrow, poor and homeless, I bear no regrets," Binh said, ensuring I understood his philosophy before he mounted the bike behind the Grab driver and sped off into the humid night.

"See you in America. Don't be a stranger," Tai said, hugging me before jumping into a taxi.

"Let's go fishing sometime," I yelled after him.

It was still hot and humid as I walked back to my brother's place. It had been fifty years since I took the familiar stroll through my old neighborhood, where I grew up and before I left for a long journey around the world. I walked by Chợ Bà Chiểu market where Má used to shop for our daily meals. The movie theater where I watched Chinese kung fu movies and Indian films was no more, now replaced with restaurants. The ancient Lăng Ông pagoda stood its ground at the corner among hundred-year-old trees, unmolested by change.

I passed by the gate of my old high school which now bears a new name. I leaned against the wall where Binh waited for me the whole day, 10 years after I left Saigon. I had come back to the place I promised to meet him, but many years too late. The grimy school building with green shutters remained the same but much smaller than I remembered it. The courtyard still smelled of Plumeria. I still heard children's laughter. Binh, Tai, and I were products of this neighborhood, this local market and this school. Just like Gia Định Quán, at least parts of us have remained.

Bulrush

Thirty years ago, I met Dr. Ni for the first time in Tràm Chim National Park where he helped the local farmers in the buffer zone with micro-financed projects. His work was always about putting the people first. He told me, "You can't protect the park and the Sarus Crane unless the people there can make a living. There will be no conservation of wildlife and their habitat if the locals are not working with you."

Over three decades, we've maintained our friendship. I've always made sure to visit him whenever I return. One time, I invited him to the U.S. to show him the research going on in the Forest Service. We were hoping to explore ways that Vietnamese farmers could get more value from Melaleuca timber, the only wood available in most of the flooded Mekong Delta. Utilization of this small timber continued to frustrate me. Without the machinery and processing technology of the U.S., farmers resorted to the only choices they had, making charcoal, building makeshift structures, and driving it into the ground to fortify foundations. Despite my good intentions, my efforts to transfer the advanced knowledge and technology wasn't helpful after all.

The gap between his world and mine was as wide as the distance between Vietnam and America, and yet we continued to try to bridge it. I kept returning with experts in ecology and land management to offer technical assistance. He showed me how things worked in the Mekong Delta, the way of the farmers with their labor, their simple methods to adapt to their changing environment—mostly through sheer perseverance.

The last time Dr. Ni and I were together, we toured the Mekong Delta for a week and he taught me all I know about its ecology and the enormous threats to its survival. I'll never forget what he said: "The Mekong Delta is a fragile ecosystem and it is threatened by three huge issues. The first is sea level rise. Do you see? Most of the land is already under water. Another half a meter and we have no place for farming. Shore erosion and salt intrusion is getting worse and worse. Second, China is building large dams upstream and water is diverted along the way, what's left for us? What will happen to the fish? And third, we are doing it to ourselves. The farmers are relying more and more on chemicals to increase yield, but it's not sustainable because they are polluting the water and the soil."

• • •

I was happy to leave Saigon for a trip to the Mekong Delta with my friend Khoa and a few Australian members of the Vietnam Foundation. I had always longed for the green and watery countryside that reminded me of the way Vietnam used to be. More than that, I was excited to see Dr. Ni again on this trip.

We headed toward Cà Mau, the southernmost province of the country. As we crossed the north fork of the Mekong River, the Aussies pointed out that the large suspension bridge was donated and built by Australia. Before that bridge was completed a decade ago, I used to cross the mighty Mekong River (both North and South forks) by ferry.

The further south we went, the more waterways I saw. Contrary to my old memories of the Delta as a fertile plain crisscrossed by canals and monkey bridges with short and rickety spans to connect people and villages, it was now a vast lake pocked with levees and small islands where people lived and farmed. Just within the last few decades, the flood zones had widened and little land remained above water, even in the rainless months.

We veered off the main highway and turned toward the coast to visit a project known as the craft village in Sóc Trăng. For miles, the road led us into even a larger waterscape. Thousands of white domesticated ducks swam and fed in the muddy water.

"Do you know that Vietnam grows the most ducks in the world?" Khoa asked me. "Second only to China, of course."

"It makes sense," I replied, impressed. "People always find a way to make a living with the land and water they have." I also remembered the lesson that Dr. Ni taught me about integrated systems that optimize the resources with plants and animals that can benefit each other. He showed me examples of farming systems such as rice and fish, greens and chicken, and many possible combinations in harmony with the rhythm of rain and dry seasons. With the booming population in the country to feed, no land would be left idle or only used for one crop, which means reliance on heavy industrial use of fertilizers and pesticides.

We got off the bus at a small village after half a day of driving. The hot mid-afternoon air welcomed us like a steam chamber.

"Hello Anh Hao, welcome back!" Dr. Ni greeted me at the roadside with that smile I have come to know so well. He hadn't changed much since the last time I saw him ten years ago. His voice was still strong and his hair had not yet turned white. Wearing sandals and an old white shirt, he was a simple man of the Delta with a Ghandi type of aura.

We hugged. "Welcome home, Anh Hao," he said the word *home* the way he had always said it whenever we met in Vietnam.

"You look good. Are you retired yet?" I asked.

"Yes, I am now a freelance operator. I am working as hard as ever though. Maybe even harder than before."

"Please help yourselves to some Nước Mía," Dr. Ni said, inviting us to a round of fresh sugarcane juice. The icy and sweet nectar hit the spot.

After Khoa made a round of introductions of his entourage, he asked Dr. Ni to give a briefing about his project. Dr. Ni led us to a quiet corner of the large warehouse so we could get away from the baking sun.

Dr. Ni began by addressing me. "Anh Hao, do you remember the last time you were here, ten years ago? We toured the area to see how the mangrove forests had come back. We also saw the development of the shrimp farming industry."

"Yes. I remember," I nodded. We'd driven by many aerated shrimp ponds, everywhere in this area.

Dr. Ni continued, "After the war, the defoliated mangrove forests grew back in this coastal part of the Mekong Delta. Unfortunately, most of them were cut down and converted to shrimp ponds. People built levees and regulated water levels in the ponds but they also disrupted the natural flow of the tidal water. At first, it was very profitable for a few years. Because of the water stagnation and the imported nitrogen rich diet, diseases set in. Heavy use of antibiotics only added to the problem. The shrimp industry crashed because the water was polluted beyond repair. It was not even possible for the farmers to go back to rice crops because the land had become too saline from salt water intrusion. Many had given up and moved away."

He had our attention now as we stood around in the warehouse. Sweat was running down my neck. Semi-transparent, corrugated, fiberglass roofs covered a one-acre structure, built with only metal pipes and plastic sheets. Inside the different compartments, bales of straws were visible in various stages of drying.

"When the temperature outside is forty degrees Celsius, the drying chamber can reach sixty. We vent it by closing and opening the plastic vents. No machinery is needed," Dr. Ni explained to us as Khoa asked about the design of the drying chambers. "This is where we dry the straw and get them ready for the basket weaving process."

Out in the yard, men and women in dark tunics milled about the big pile of fresh green straws that were recently brought in. They hand-carried bundles into the drying chambers. I discretely stole a few pictures of them with my camera. They were local farmers toiling in the heat and I was with a group of foreigners in designer field clothes making observations of their livelihood. Who gave me the right to be so distant from my own people, I wondered.

"What is this straw we are looking at?" I asked, trying to divert myself from the sense of guilt.

"It is bulrush, a local water plant of the sedge family. Did you see the green fields on the way here? They grow everywhere."

Indeed, I saw fields of tall grass swaying in the wind in abandoned paddies. I first thought it was a type of cattail but it is not— no cylindrical, corn dog spikes.

"The farmers harvest the bulrush and bring it here to wash and dry. Others come to pick up the dried straws and weave baskets with them. Then they bring the baskets back to the warehouse to be sent to different markets."

I noticed piles of steel wire molds used as models for various types of baskets. In another section, intricate and beautiful laundry and storage baskets for household use waited to be shipped.

Dr. Ni continued, "You can't believe how little money we needed to get started. We did this with local labor and cheap material, before we got any investment funding from the Vietnam Foundation. But first, you have to convince the farmers to do it. That's the hardest part."

"As the land was being abandoned, I observed that the bulrush sedge was the only vegetation that could grow in the brackish wetlands, and it thrived. I started a pilot project to demonstrate to the farmers that they could harvest the bulrush, wash and dry it, and weave baskets with the tough fibrous material. The bulrush worked even better than the water hyacinth that also grows here like a weed. I convinced the farmers to form a co-op and build a cottage industry with the bulrush-to-basket plan. If sustainable, this could provide enough jobs and clean the environment so they don't have to leave their homes to seek employment in the city."

"The co-op now has about five thousand farmers who are involved in one way or another in the project. Many weavers are women and old folks. Even just weaving five baskets a day, laborers earn around five dollars, enough to buy food for their families in this rural area."

"So where do the baskets go? Who buys them?" I had to ask.

"We found a company with markets in Saigon and overseas. They are selling our products in Walmart in the U.S. The loop is now complete—supply, labor force, and market."

"How about shrimp and fish, do they coexist with the bulrush?" Khoa asked.

"Yes, the bulrush thrives in brackish water and cleans the water and soil. There is plenty of clean water around the plants for fish and shrimp to live naturally. The bulrush regenerates itself from its root mass, we don't have to do anything after we harvest the stems. It grows back all on its own. It sequesters carbon both above and below the ground, a good measure for climate change mitigation."

•••

"Anh Ni, I have a gift for you," I said when he was done with the presentation. "This book of stories is about my love for the Vietnamese people and the land. One chapter in it is about you."

I had brought with me a signed copy of my book *Skinny Woman in a Straw Hat* to give him personally. Dr. Ni came over to where I stood in the circle and embraced me. We both were overcome with tears.

"To know Dr. Ni is to understand the heart and soul of the Mekong Delta," I told the group in my shaking voice.

It took a couple of minutes before Dr. Ni regained his composure. Still with his arm around my shoulder, he told a story about us.

"Many years ago, Dr. Hao invited me to the U.S. to learn about research in the Forest Service. When I left to return home, he gave the rest of the grant money to me and told me to do something good with it. I think he was trying to help me because he thought I was poor. Years passed, and he had never asked me for a report of what I did with the money. When he came back ten years ago, I had a chance to show him what I did with it. I took him to Hòa An, a poor village that he'd visited with me on one of his trips. Now there is a school for kids there. The money he gave me was used as seed money to build that school. Education is what the farmers need for their kids to do better. They have no excuse now."

I'd never expected that from Dr. Ni and that's what I love about him. In a land of endemic corruption, he didn't pocket the money for himself, although I would have been fine with that. Instead, he honored our friendship beyond my expectations.

It was later in the day and the delegation had to reach another destination before dark. As we were about to board the bus, the clouds gathered and heavy rain drops fell on the plexiglass roofs. Wind swept water sideways against the clear plastic walls. The farmers rushed out and hurriedly moved the piles of straw from the yard to the warehouse. Everything was done by their hands, rain or shine.

I hugged Dr. Ni goodbye. He said, "You are always in my heart, Anh Hao. I am a man of few words, but you know I will always remember you."

We drove away from Sóc Trăng and headed further south to the tip of Cà Mau. Along the road, I saw water everywhere. Ducks frolicked in the waterscape among patches of green bulrush waving in the breeze. What used to be mangrove forests were gone forever, not by defoliation and napalm anymore, but by the failed shrimp farm business.

The Sóc Trăng project is nothing short of a miracle. Dr. Ni showed me again that sustainability is not just a fancy word and marketing tool, it is a lofty but achievable goal when you can balance ecological, social and economic elements together like this. However, I wonder how long this project will be viable with further sea level rise, the fluctuations in the world market, and the pressure for more food and shelter for the country.

The Mekong River originates from the snow packs in the Himalayas and Tibetan plateau and runs through China, Myanmar, Thailand, Laos, and Cambodia before reaching the Delta. It has been the lifeblood not only for the people in the Delta but for the whole country. The Mekong Delta is the rice basket of Vietnam. The Mekong River is now at the mercy of dam and canal constructions upstream and the ongoing threat of sea level rise. Will there be another bulrush to save the locals from displacement? Will there be another Dr. Ni to save the day?

Out the bus window, the green fields calmed my mind. I thought of the song, *Để Gió Cuốn Đi* by Trịnh Công Sơn. The lyrics spoke so much about Dr. Ni:

In life, you must have heart
Do you know what for?
Let it go, let the wind carry
Clouds over the river
Over day, over night
Let your heart go with the time
When evening comes, you need laughter
Let sorrows fall with dead leaves
In the streams
In the morning you hear the birds sing
Their songs in the wind
You will love tomorrow no matter how weary
Be happy, my friend

Monkey Bridges

Khoa sent me an email invitation: "You are invited to attend the opening ceremony for Bridge 29 in Cà Mau,"

"Sounds very interesting," I replied. What's this Bridge 29?"

"The Vietnam Foundation in Australia is helping the Cà Mau province replace the rickety monkey bridges with concrete ones."

"There goes another cultural icon," I replied with a wink emoji. "Maybe we should save one and donate it to the Smithsonian, before they are gone for good."

As far as I remember, these monkey bridges dotted the landscape in the Mekong Delta. Every time I looked down the canals and rivers, I saw makeshift bridges made of coconut tree trunks buttressed by bamboo poles. In the flooded areas of the Delta where big trees don't grow, coconut and bamboo are the only building materials. People balance themselves on shaky and slippery stems, hands on a bamboo handrail as they dance with the wind. Some of them even carry heavy baskets of fruit and vegetables on a shoulder stick as they cross over the water. Wooden boats pass underneath them. Water hyacinth drifts aimlessly along with the ebb and flow of the tides. Thatched huts and bamboo groves line the banks of canals as in a classic painting of the peaceful life in the Mekong Delta.

The idea of building concrete bridges to replace monkey bridges in the Mekong Delta intrigued me and I decided to spend a few days with Khoa and members of the Vietnam Foundation to witness this transition.

• • •

After a long day of driving, we arrived at our destination, the remotest province in the Delta, which my father called "the end of the earth." Cà Mau had a terrible reputation back when I was still a child growing up in Saigon. Bad poems depicted the deplorable conditions of a god-forsaken place, where mosquitoes sang like bamboo flutes and leeches squirmed like flat noodles. It was not true anymore. As we drove in the province capital of Cà Mau, brand new palatial government buildings and imposing military cemeteries lined the main boulevard, all gated and surrounded by manicured gardens. Newly planted trees lined the roads wide enough for large trucks to rumble through. The city had become modernized like a new Saigon, only cleaner and better planned.

We pulled into the 4-star hotel Muong Thanh at the center of Cà Mau City in the late afternoon. I couldn't believe my eyes. The lobby of this hotel was large enough to hangar a Boeing 737. A hundred young boys in white shirts and girls in blue Áo Dài were taking selfies in front of the spacious restaurant and conference rooms. They must have been students in a hospitality school on a field trip to learn how a luxury hotel operates.

It was still early afternoon when we checked in the hotel and I had one hour to spare before we regrouped for dinner. I took a walk around the public square in front of the hotel to take some pictures of the town. Large and colorful banners with giant crustacean images announced the upcoming Shrimp Festival. A large crowd gathered around an outdoor stage practicing and rehearsing for the show to celebrate the miracle of Cà Mau's success.

The shrimp industry had transformed Cà Mau from the dreaded backwater province to a wealthy region, at least for the seat of the provincial government. During the war, all the mangrove forests were defoliated and burned. After the fall of Saigon, the forests recovered on their own for about twenty years and then were destroyed again, this time by the people and their need for farm land. They cut down the mangroves, dug ponds, and built levees to raise shrimp industrially. Cà Mau province is among the largest producers and exporters of tiger shrimp in the world.

• • •

I met up with Khoa and other members of the Vietnam Foundation in the lobby at 6:00 pm to meet with our hosts, the women of the Cà Mau Buddhist Association.

"I made a mistake," Khoa confided in me as we stood around. "I invited the Australian Consulate General from Saigon to the bridge opening event, on behalf of the Vietnam Foundation."

"So, what's wrong with that?"

"I wanted to build support for the Foundation, since it started out as a non-profit in Australia. Little did I know this ceremony has gotten out of hand."

"I see. How bad is it?"

"First, I thought the event would be a friendly meeting with only our hosts and partners, the women in the Buddhist Association. Since the provincial government is now aware that the Australian Consulate is coming, they wanted to show up too even though they have not funded the bridge project. We will have the government officials and even the media there. I am not ready for this level of attention. I don't need the fanfare."

"Don't worry. We can do this," I assured Khoa now that there was nothing we could do about the guest list.

The province government had already demanded to know all our names and passport information when we arrived. They also issued a two-page program with names and titles of all the local dignitaries who would be making speeches at the event. All of this would be televised by Cà Mau TV.

The women of the Cà Mau Buddhist Association arrived at the hotel lobby to meet and greet us. In their fifties and sixties, these ladies devote their time and energy to charity work as their main activity. Tuyết, the ringleader, shook hands with the Australians and hugged us Vietnamese expats. Her loud laughter was so infectious I felt an instant connection with her like a sister I never had.

"Welcome to Cà Mau," she smiled broadly at Khoa and me. "Thank you. It is so wonderful to have friends from overseas coming to help the farmers here. We have a lot to show you tomorrow, but tonight, we have a feast for you. The best seafood in Vietnam."

Sarah, the Australian Consulate General from Saigon,, arrived with a Vietnamese translator who looked very much like my niece. I was immediately impressed with Sarah, a tall blonde lady in a simple dress and without makeup, who spoke with the Australian accent that I had long forgotten. After everyone had been accounted for, we drove to the largest seafood restaurant in town.

A long table at the center of the large open-air restaurant had been reserved for us. Glass tanks of live fish and tiger shrimp lined the walls. All eyes were on Sarah since she was the dignitary representing Australia and the reason for the provincial government to get all excited. The rest of us were now supporting actors and props for the show.

After a round of formal introductions of all attendees, the Cà Mau ladies played a video presentation on the big screen about the bridge project. The YouTube production began with the heart-touching music of *Làng Tôi* with a soaring and soulful bamboo flute. The song painted a scene of the village banyan tree, a meandering river, thatched roofs, bamboo hedges, and areca palms. It went on about the fire and smoke of war, and the sojourner longing for the day to return home.

Then the video pivoted to an interview with a skinny and frail Vietnamese grandmother. "I can't cross the bridge anymore with this leg," she said while tapping her knee. The camera panned to a monkey bridge that I wouldn't dare cross even in my good shape. Children floated in makeshift rafts made of Styrofoam coolers, hanging on to guide ropes to get to their school on the other side of the river. The drone images of the inundated landscape seen from above made me wonder: how could people cope if the sea level continued to rise? At the end of the song, I was almost in tears.

Sarah stood up and spoke briefly before we began the banquet. As expected of a diplomat, it was a speech to thank everyone, but I was impressed with what she also said. "Australia and Vietnam have enjoyed a long and deep connection. We began our relations in 1973 and we have maintained our friendship ever since. Let's toast to another fifty years of collaboration."

She was referring to the Paris Agreement in 1973 between North Vietnam and the U.S. While the U.S. disowned the war and walked away, Australia did something amazing: she promptly established diplomatic relations with Hanoi. As far as I know, Australia may be the first and only country of all the U.S. allies that did so. I was a student in Canberra when this happened and for a short time before the fall of Saigon in April 1975, there were both North and South Vietnamese embassies there. Sometimes, hostility broke out between North and South Vietnamese in the streets when we ran into each other. After all, we were supposed to be enemies.

I found a quiet moment to speak to Sarah and presented her with a signed copy of my book *Skinny Woman in a Straw Hat*.

"This book embodies my love for the people and the land. I hope you enjoy it. One story is about the time I went to Australia fifty years ago. I was a Colombo Plan student but I didn't stay there long. Please accept my thanks. Thank you, Australia!"

I am glad I had the chance to do that before the beer and the food arrived. The women of the Buddhist Association were loud and hospitable. They made sure we ate the soft-shelled crabs and the big broiled shrimp. They heaped chopped vegetables and fish into the boiling hotpots to cook for us and filled our glasses with more beer.

"Một Hai Ba Dzô!" They chanted—*One, Two, Three, Drink!*— every time someone made a toast.

Tuyết and the hosts put on quite a show. Not only did they make sure we were well supplied with food and beer, they entertained us with karaoke singing. One by one, each woman took the stage to sing a song about their home and love for the land. Actually, they were good singers—they must have had lots of practice.

"C'mon. Please sing something for us," Tuyết dragged me to the stage.

I went along and belted out a song. It wasn't American Idol material, but at least I reciprocated. Soon enough, everyone got up to the stage and sang together, songs about our love for the land.

It was getting late but the hosts were just warming up. Sarah had been huddling with her translator over incoming messages on her phone. Something important must have happened and a person in her position must respond. She did her best to show interest in all the singing on stage but finally, she tapped her helper on the shoulder. "Party is over," the translator announced to us in her sweet voice.

After Sarah left, we stayed around for a while longer with our hosts. Not only could the women of Cà Mau drink, they sure could flirt. They took selfies of with us, one by one, before saying good night.

"I hope these pictures don't show up on Facebook," I joked.

"Cà Mau women are very friendly and cute," an older lady was playing with me. It was a well-known line in one of the local songs.

"It's too late," I showed her my wedding ring.

"It's not too late, Anh Hao," she laughed out loud.

"Thank you for your food, your singing, and your care for the people and the land."

"Please come back. We need your help." She embraced me like a sister.

Reluctantly, the Buddhist ladies let us go back to the hotel. It was only 10:00 pm. I bet they thought of us as party poopers.

● ● ●

To get to Bridge 29 the next day, we boarded a couple of long and low wooden motor boats and cruised down river. We passed under many bridges in disrepair or downright decommissioned. The whole structures were gone except for the concrete piers that stuck out from the muddy river banks. In contrast to the luxurious

4-star hotel and the ostentatious government buildings in Cà Mau City, this place along the river was totally devoid of infrastructure improvements. The further away from the provincial seat, the more desolate the villages became, as if they had not benefited at all from the wealth generated by the shrimp industry.

The half-hour ride ended up at a small village, and a large crowd had been there waiting for us under a tent shelter. As forewarned, the bridge opening ceremony was no longer the small and intimate event Khoa had originally intended. The local TV crews were setting up tripods and cameras. Several government officials in white shirts and black pants sat up front reviewing their speeches. The Buddhist women donned their best and most colorful Áo Dài. Two dozen school kids around the age of twelve had been sitting in the tent since 8:00 am and it was getting hot. Dang hot. The school teacher puffed on a cigarette, blowing smoke across the tent, while the students stayed quiet and respectful.

The foot bridge had been completed and people had been walking and riding their bikes across it already. Red, yellow, and green flags adorned the bridge every few feet. Painted green and white to represent Australia, the arc spanned at least 90 feet over the river.

We stood around for almost an hour while the TV guys screwed around with the stereo loudspeakers to test them. They moved the podium back and forth to make sure they could have a clear shot of the dignitaries.

Then the ceremony began, around 10:00 am. It started with the province level, Chairman or Vice-Chair, I am not sure. He read off about two pages of text while Sarah's translator gave us the English version line by line. At one point, the loudspeakers didn't work, so he started all over again, from the top.

Someone led the applause every few minutes, as scripted in the program that they had passed out to us the day before. The speech, as always, began with thanks to the national communist party and pleasantries to all the distinguished guests. He went on at great lengths about the transformation of Ca Mau from a poor province to the booming shrimp capital of the country. I listened carefully for any part about what the provincial government had done to help the farmers with the new bridges. There was none. Then the Mayor of Cà Mau City got up to thank the Chairman of the province, the Buddhist Women Committee, Sarah, and the Vietnam Foundation, before delivering another canned speech, with translation of course. Again, this speech was not much different from the one I had heard earlier.

Amazingly, the children remained stoically quiet despite the cigarette smoke drifting through the tent. None of them got up to go to the bathroom the entire time.

I couldn't take the heat under the tent so I sneaked out the back, taking pictures of the mudskippers in the river bank. By the time I checked back in with the program, the Buddhist women were up next. They had been managing the bridge projects with the donation money from the Vietnam Foundation. As Dr. Ni had told me before: "Never give money to the men because they will drink and gamble it all. The women will get things done for the kids and the community."

Tuyết summarized the work, "We have built dozens of bridges with the finance from various charity organizations and individuals. The experience has enabled us to fine-tune the process so much that our construction cost is probably the lowest in the whole country. A small 25 m bridge (75 feet) costs just 80 million Vietnam Dongs (3,500 dollars). The donation is used solely for materials and labor. The Cà Mau Buddhist Organization has our own volunteer bridge design team and project managers. Some of us travel at our own expenses to remote communities to assess the need for a bridge. Then we make sure they are built like this."

Khoa told me about the donations, "The Vietnam Foundation has financed a total of 25 bridges. Another 10 are planned for next year. The bridges don't just make it easier for the children to go to school, they help save lives when people need urgent medical help. Farmers can bring their goods to the market more efficiently. Even the dogs enjoy the bridge since they don't have to swim across the creeks and get covered in mud."

Then it was time for Sarah to speak. She had been patiently waiting her turn for an hour and a half. Near midday, sweat was rolling down her pale face. Still smiling, she delivered a short speech. After the obligatory pleasantries, she gave the message that I had heard the previous day.

"I am proud of the enduring relationship that our two countries have enjoyed over the last fifty years. I am looking forward to the next fifty."

After all the speeches had been delivered and taped, Sarah helped hand out gifts to the kids who had patiently been waiting four hours to stand up. They each received a backpack and the equivalent of five dollars from the Vietnam Foundation. That made them very happy. They didn't get to do this every day.

For the camera, long red ribbons were spread out across many dignitary hands which cut them into chunks simultaneously with large scissors. Then we were free to walk across the bridge.

It was nice to get away from oppressive heat in the tent. Following the crowd, I went up the steep climb to the crown of the bridge and looked down the river. It's not the iconic canal and village view of the classical painting in my head. I saw a vast ocean of silty water and a few strips of land. A strong breeze cooled me off and it smelled of sea water mixed with the mud of the Mekong River.

Khoa stood next to me as we looked around at the waterscape. I asked Khoa the question that has been on my mind: "This province is so rich off the shrimp business. How come they rely on our donations to build bridges? It seems to me they could easily pay for them the way they built hotels and government buildings."

Khoa nodded. "It is obvious, isn't it? Our rulers have never taken care of the poor. That's the way it has always been for thousands of years starting with the kings and their courts and now the ruling class. But I love working with the Buddhist women here. They really mean well. At least, we are doing some good."

Then I asked a follow-up question: "How many bridges will be enough? These are not just to replace monkey bridges. We are talking long spans, a hundred feet or more. How will they keep up with inundation and climate change?"

Khoa had no answer, but I heard what he didn't say: *We bail. We do the best we can while the boat is sinking.*

The Reunion

The Colombo Plan group was plotting a fifty-year reunion. For the venue, Khoa and the planning team posed three options:

Vietnam, where we began

Sydney, where we spent the first summer together

A pleasure cruise around Southeast Asia

Decision was made by popular vote: we were to meet in Vietnam. Our Colombo Plan 73 cohort would have its 50th anniversary in Hồ Tràm, a beach resort not far from Saigon.

Sometime back in 1955 (the year I was born), six countries including Australia and New Zealand got together in Colombo, capital of Ceylon (now Sri Lanka) and agreed to sponsor kids from war-torn countries, train them, and return them to rebuild their homelands.

From 1955 to 1975, Australia took in nearly 600 students from Vietnam and I was one of them. Incidentally, about 600 Australian soldiers perished in Vietnam fighting in a war alongside America and other allies. It was an amazing symmetry in the number of souls lost and saved.

In life, a defining moment can change our lives completely. For my Colombo Plan group, it was that day fifty years ago. On the concrete pad outside Tân Sơn Nhất Airport, I was among dozens of nervous kids saying goodbye to their parents, siblings and friends. The boys donned tailor-made suits, neckties, and new shoes. The girls in their best Áo Dài. I had no suit jacket, only a new white shirt, brown polyester pants, fake leather belt and shoes, uncomfortable in the chokehold of a stiff necktie.

On one of the Zoom meetings with Khoa and the planning team, I had a proposal:

"Let's put together something to commemorate this momentous event. Each one of us can share something like a photo or a story, or maybe an item that reminds us of the time we left Saigon. Then we will put all that together in a book of memories. I am willing to be the coordinator and editor to capture the collective memory of this group and how our lives have turned out since."

I heard many voice votes of approval for the idea and was excited about the anthology we planned to produce after the trip.

● ● ●

Before the reunion, Khoa and I traveled through the Mekong Delta together for a few days. He is the only friend from the Colombo Plan cohort that I had kept close contact with through the years.

"About the reunion, I don't think I still know anyone. I wasn't in Australia long enough to bond with you guys. After the first summer in Sydney, I went to Canberra and then to America not long after." I confessed.

"Mai will be there," Khoa said.

"That's great. I would love to see her."

At least, there would be one I knew well. Mai and I were the only two going to Canberra together, to the same university. All the others stayed in Sydney, or went to Melbourne or Adelaide. The first few months, Mai and I were lonely and found company in each other. Our cohorts thought that we would pair up but we drifted apart as each found our own love interests.

When I arrived at the rendezvous location in downtown Saigon to catch the shuttle bus for the Hồ Tràm resort, a few of the Colombo Plan colleagues were waiting there. I had a little trouble with names and faces but I recognized Mai right away because she had hardly changed at all. She was with her husband John whom I had met back when I was still in Canberra. Both of them were skinny and tall, and elegantly dressed.

"You look great!" I complimented Mai. "No change at all."

"You too! You look taller, and you have changed a lot. I don't think I could recognize you if we met somewhere in the street." She twittered like a bird, just the same way she was fifty years back.

"Really? I was just a kid back then. I could have grown an inch, tops. However, I have added fifty pounds."

John passed his hand over his head, as bald as mine. "Chrome domes!" he laughed.

Mai added, "Yes, we are older now. But I am still young at heart. Where is your sweetheart?"

I said as we boarded the bus, "Diep wants to give me the freedom to move about. She doesn't travel well these days."

It took two hours to reach the beach resort through sixty miles of chaotic traffic and continuous urban expansion. On this high-speed freeway, traffic only moved at thirty miles an hour because we had to share the roads with oxcarts and mopeds. Occasionally, people and chickens crossed the road. Wherever there are roads, there are houses. In Vietnam, people prefer to build right next to the road so they can open shops and restaurants, and sometimes just to be on high solid grounds. Beyond the houses, you still see green farms and rice fields. Every inch of ground is used and if vacant, plastic bags and Styrofoam cups collect. Every now and then, an open pit garbage dump smolders in a cloud of acrid smoke.

As we approached the beach resort, the landscape changed abruptly. Coconut trees bent in the wind against the backdrop of the blue ocean and white sandy beach like any resort in Honolulu. A manicured golf course buffered the hotel from the rest of the world outside. Compared with the squalor that our bus drove through to get to this heaven, it was a shocking contrast and as an ecologist, I saw Hồ Tràm as a fresh scar on the landscape.

• • •

One by one, old friends arrived and checked in the palatial hotel. I heard the Aussie accent on most of them as we milled around the grand lobby. They had done well with their time in Australia and America, all retired and enjoying the golden years with travels, tennis, and golf.

They looked good. Half the men went bald, like me. The ladies aged well with only a few wrinkles and bad knees. After a buffet dinner in the casino, we had a night of rest on our own before the reunion the next day. I avoided the small group gatherings and retreated to the comfort of my room. The next morning, I woke up as the sun rose over the ocean. From my hotel window, the vista was like a postcard, with blue sky, red sun, green vegetation, and a pristine beach. The venue couldn't have been nicer or cleaner. Unlike the rest of Vietnam, there was no traffic or trash anywhere in sight. The only thing that reminded me of the world outside of the resort were the workers in gray tunics and conical straw hats picking up every leaf that dropped on the lawns. A tractor combed the sand every morning to make the beach look like a massive zen garden.

The reunion with the Colombo Plan was to take place in the evening. However, small groups had already formed and at one point all of us gathered by the pool for group pictures in our newly made Hồ Tràm t-shirts. We also had a Zoom meeting in Khoa's room for the ones who couldn't show up.

Mai and I found ourselves alone as John swam laps in the Olympic-sized pool. We relaxed in lawn chairs facing the calm beach and ocean beyond.

"Gosh! It has been a long time, fifty years already," Mai primed the pump.

"I still remember those years in Canberra. You know, I was really happy there. I never thought I would leave Australia, unless to go back to Vietnam."

Then she laughed, "We had them fooled for a while. The Sydney gang believed that you and I would hook up together. What really happened there?"

"Nothing happened between us," I said. "We lived in different dorms on campus. We met once in a while to walk to class, but I wasn't ready for any commitment. I had nothing to offer."

"It's not that. You were always sad and quiet. You never said anything about how you felt. Nothing. Back then, you were a mystery."

I nodded my head in agreement, "I am sorry I was no fun. You, however, were blooming like a rose in the new world, having a time of your life."

Her voice rose to a higher twitter, "Yes! I was free for the first time in my life to live the way I wanted, not constrained by my family and the Vietnamese society that put so much expectations on girls to comply, to walk a few steps behind a man, to nod and obey. In Australia, I got to choose whom I wanted to be my partner."

"And you met John in the same dorm. He was very attentive to you," I recalled.

"My parents in Vietnam would not have approved, but I was in Australia now. Besides, can I tell you the truth?"

"Yes, it is good for the soul."

"I am not attracted to Asian men. I never was," she said.

I couldn't blame her. We Asian men have always had a low image in the media and in real life. We are never portrayed well as leading men in movies, always the angry and vengeful martial artists at best, and ugly villains at worst.

"I understand. I often felt inadequate. I was skinny, short, inarticulate, and poor. I have gained a lot more confidence since—but back then, sheesh!"

She laughed again, "But you got the most beautiful Vietnamese girl to fall in love with you. How did you do that? All the other boys were jealous."

"I didn't do anything. We met her at the first Christmas party at the Embassy and the rest just happened."

"You were the saddest boy I had ever seen," Mai said. "Maybe she fell for that. You were so homesick, and you didn't flirt like the other guys. So what really happened? Why did you leave Canberra?"

I told Mai our story. "When Saigon fell, her parents decided to migrate to the U.S. where they had wanted to live. Diep was supposed to go with them as a family package. I thought we would say goodbye and make promises to find each other again in a few years after I finished my training."

"That would be difficult. It's a long way between Australia and America, and who knows if anyone can wait for years." Mai said.

"I had no idea when I could make it to America to see her, but the following Sunday when I went to visit her family, her parents told me to take good care of her. She was going to stay behind with me and they made me promise to marry her. The end of that year, we got married. It was a small quiet church wedding without family on either side."

"I remember that. You didn't invite anyone. Not even me." She looked at me with sad eyes.

"We had not even finished school. We had no money, no jobs, no idea about the future. All we had was each other when we got married." I told her the rest of the story, "One year later, we saved enough money for airline tickets to visit her parents in San Francisco. It was supposed to be a four-week trip but it turned out to be another life-long adventure. We never used the return tickets, and became American citizens ten years later."

"It looks like you two have made a good life for yourselves in America," Mai brought me out of the reverie and back to the present.

"You too. Having great kids, retired, sailing the world. Not bad at all!" I was truly happy for her.

Mai reminded me again, "You and Diep were the most romantic couple on campus, like Romeo and Juliet."

I agreed, "We were two kids in love. We just followed our hearts."

"You left so suddenly, without saying goodbye." It sounded like a reprimand. Mai ordered two more Mai Tais and we sipped them in silence, enjoying the view of the blue South China Sea.

• • •

At sunset, I arrived at the dining hall for the grand reunion. The girls showed up in silk Áo Dài and the guys in their casual and colorful Hawaiian shirts. Dinner was grand with tiger shrimp, lobster, and roast beef served by local young waitresses. After dinner, everyone took the stage to tell stories, jokes, and memorable moments in their lives.

"We are a special group," Mai said in her meadowlark voice. "The Colombo Plan picked the best kids of our time, and we are lucky to be here today. I am so thankful to Australia for this life."

Khoa made a presentation about our visits to Sóc Trăng and Cà Mau. He had become the spokesperson for the Vietnam Foundation and wasted no time in promoting the cause.

Unlike me, Khoa is not bothered by the way Vietnam is changing. He sees changes as inevitable while I resist them. He runs a small IT company with many Vietnamese employees and is well connected in Saigon. For as long as I have known him, he has been politically savvy and can get along with anyone. Had he been given an opportunity to serve, he could have been a successful politician in the new Vietnam.

John, a jovial kind of guy, told a classic lawyer joke and it was still funny because of the way he told it—something about an engineer going to hell after he died. He made so many improvements to the living conditions there that God in Heaven complained to Satan, threatening to sue him for breach of contract. "Good luck with finding a lawyer up there," the Devil replied.

They put together a slideshow to remind us of how dorky we looked fifty years ago and how many children and grandchildren had been born since.

Khoa asked me to talk about my book *Skinny Woman in a Straw Hat*, which I had just published. The book is a collection of short stories about the love I have for the Vietnamese people and the land. I read the first few lines in the introduction to the book.

"Vietnam is a woman, a long-suffering mother," my history teacher pointed at the map on the high school wall. "Look at her: up north, the mountainous border is a conical straw hat to keep her safe from China's endless assaults. Her thin neck is a stretch of sand between the Pacific Ocean and the Ho Chi Minh Trail along the mountain range. Her belly is the central highland that has been the home of many tribes, now taken over by colonial greed for coffee and tea plantations. The Mekong Delta is the rice basket that barely feeds the whole country. Look again: she is doubled over from all this pain and sorrow of war."

Moved by my own words, I quietly sat down. Silence took over the room. I heard no comments or feedback afterwards, like it never happened.

After a few minutes of awkwardness, the festivity continued. Mai and the ladies entertained us with a few songs from the days in Sydney when we were kids with dreams in our heads and homesickness in our hearts.

Late in the night, the party had to end. My friends seemed satisfied with the event as we said goodnight after a few more group pictures. They were totally at peace, a happy-go-lucky gang who can have a good time, while I still look back and mourn the twenty years I lost. I agonize over the environmental issues facing this country and abhor the obscene gap between the rich and the poor, the contrast between the Hồ Tràm resort and the rest of the Mekong Delta. Lucky for my friends in Australia, they didn't miss Vietnam much since they had always maintained close relations with our home country. They don't carry the baggage that I do.

● ● ●

The next morning, I got up early and walked around the hotel gardens alone with my camera to snap pictures of the Sunbirds feeding on the flowers and the Bulbuls nesting in the coconut trees. I was glad to find a quiet moment with nature, even in the most unnatural place.

After the morning bird walk, I got to breakfast after everyone had already finished their attack on the buffet spread.

Mai asked where I was. "We looked for you. Did you cry last night?"

"Yes, I get emotional whenever I read from my book. You know, my Vietnam stories capture all my love for the people and the land."

She said, "You have always been that way. The same sad little boy as back then. For me, I only look forward and Australia is my home now. I am just a tourist here."

"Maybe we haven't really changed all that much. We are still the same people we were fifty years ago. Only older."

She said goodbye. "Please take care. Hi to Diep."

We took a few more group pictures and checked out. Our farewell was swift. Some of us went on to other tourist destinations, while some stayed for a few more days at the beautiful Hồ Tràm resort and casino. I took the shuttle bus back to Saigon and then a taxi ride back to my brother's place in the alley.

That was the last time I saw my Colombo Plan cohorts. The book of memories I suggested has not happened and no one asked for it. Other than Khoa, I haven't heard from my other cohorts since.

The Mango Tree

"Starting a new life," my brother Hòa messaged me, with a picture of him and a younger woman in the background.

Good for him, I thought. It has been at least twenty years since Phương died, and he had not remarried. Now in his sixties, he deserves some happiness. Many women in his village church had tried to net him and finally someone did.

I gave the driver the address to Hòa's village and he entered it in his cell phone. Google Maps would take us there, he assured me. The once dirt road to the village has now turned into a busy thoroughfare with heavy traffic going in both directions. Trucks loaded with rice, sweet potato, sugar cane, and coconuts headed east to Saigon, the empty ones the other direction. I recognized the landmarks when we got close to the farm: the school, the church, and the canal. New houses, mostly large ones with iron gates, had sprung up and lined the whole road. What used to be my brother's distinct farm house near the canal was not easy to spot anymore.

We stopped the car and asked a street vendor about Mr. Hòa, the mango farmer, and right away she pointed at the gate two houses down. His house is a bit recessed from the road and we had driven past it.

The dogs barked as we pulled into the gravel driveway. Hòa came out to greet us. He had not changed much except all his hair had turned gray, the color of his clouded eyes. He was still skinny and lank, although a lot less muscular than he used to be.

He introduced me to his new wife. "This is Hương."

"Sounds familiar," I made an attempt at humor about rhyming with Phương, his late wife's name. It wasn't lost on him.

I bowed and offered my congratulations. She didn't seem shy, just giving me a half smile, conscious of her overbite.

Hòa said, waving his arm, "Come on in. You can stay in the air-conditioned room, where you stayed before. The bathroom in the back is all yours."

The farmhouse still looked the same, as Hòa had not spent any money on home improvement or building an impressive villa like his neighbors. The front of the house where Má used to live was now set aside as the altar with pictures of our four grandparents, Ba and Má, and Phương. Hòa always had flowers and fruits for the deceased. The back of the house was for Hòa's daughter Xiu, her husband and their two little girls, temporarily displaced by my presence.

Hòa read my mind as I was eyeing the large mango tree looming over the courtyard. "It's fifty years old now. The oldest and the sweetest. We still get a ton of mangoes from it every year."

I used to sit under this mango tree with Má to watch Hòa and Phương work and their children play. We shared family dinners under the shelter of this tree in the kerosene lamp light before the village was electrified.

I inspected the large tree trunk, now darkened and covered with green moss. A few large branches had been lobbed off because of rot. It was only a few years old when I returned to the farm for the first time. Má planted it from a seed and it germinated and grew. It had witnessed the lives of my family who were banished to the new-economic zone of Tay Ninh after the fall of Saigon. They cleared the jungle, planted cassava and cashew trees at first. When the soil improved and water was brought in through a newly dug canal, Hòa planted mango trees and built up from there. He bought every acre of land that his neighbors abandoned as they gave up on the pioneer life in the new-economic zone.

●●●

Later in the day, Hòa and Hương, Xiu's family and I ate dinner under the tree as we always did. They treated me to steamed rice with the classic dishes: fried fish, boiled vegetables dipped in a thick cooked fish sauce, and my favorite pumpkin soup. However, something was missing.

"Where are Ti and Thao?" I asked. Xiu's son and daughter-in-law used to share these quarters.

"They are taking care of the other place and prefer to live there."

Hòa's farm has two large tracts. The original piece is where he lives and the larger one was purchased later. It's a mile away, near the church cemetery. Ti and his family were living there now.

"Ti hasn't been happy since I remarried. I am sorry to say," Hòa said.

"Maybe he misses his mother. Give him time," I ventured to guess.

"It has been twenty years since Phương died. I didn't want to remarry, but I got a bit lonely at times. You just can't make logical decisions all the time." It sounded like an apology.

I looked into his gray eyes. "I am happy for you, brother."

Hòa lowered his voice, "He hasn't talked to me since he and his family moved out. We haven't had a meal together since."

"Do you know why?" I asked.

"It's complicated. Maybe you should talk to him. He will love to see you."

"Tomorrow, I will go to the cemetery in the morning and then I will stop by to visit with Ti," I said before getting up from the table.

●●●

Ti was a cheerful ten-year old when I returned here for the first time. I watched him turn from a normal happy kid to a quiet adolescent then to an antisocial adult. Every year or two when I came to visit, he talked less and less. He only stopped by to light a cigarette and then got lost again in the rows of mango trees. In his happy moments, he brought me a fresh coconut with a straw for me to sip and sat with me for a while.

I often wondered if he would have turned out differently had he not been so attached to Má, my mother and his grandmother. Má constantly needed company and he was her "tail." He followed her everywhere like a baby chick after mother hen. Without a son to lean on all the time, Má took on Ti as her dependent, her companion, her servant, and her pet. She rewarded him with treats and talked to him constantly about every grievance she had, day in and day out through his teenage years. His demeanor took on hers, like the sad eyes and lack of interest in games and sports that other teenagers played. The two were inseparable and there was nothing Hòa and Phương could do about it, knowing it wasn't healthy for their son.

His sister told me that he had no friends, and certainly no girlfriend. Several girls in the village thought he was handsome but he had no interest in any of them. He fell in love with a girl much older than him, but she later went to the seminary and became a nun. He swore he would not find another love, ever.

If Má lived in America and was properly diagnosed, I believe she would be treated for severe depression. Caring for seven sons in a time of war without much help from a wayward husband probably did her in. She was happy for a while when I returned from afar and I thought with my support, she would no longer have to worry about money and she would enjoy her old age in comfort. That joy didn't last long and she kept bringing up sad stories and the sorrows that weighed heavy on her body and soul. It was painful to be with her and watch the dark forces circling over her waking moments.

"Ti needs me. Someone has to teach him how to become a strong person. People are like bamboo stems. You can only shape them when they are young. I did that with you and look at what you have become." She said this every time I told her that she was smothering Ti and he needed to be with other kids his age. He had no friends nor hobbies. He was with her all day long, as she wished.

I was very concerned about his future because there wasn't a very good school in the village so I arranged to have him stay with my other brother in Saigon. He could go to school there and hang out with Ni, his cousin of the same age.

When I watched the two kids play together at the farm, they were like two puppies. They went swimming with me in the canal, picked water lilies, and flew the kite in the field. They could have passed as twins. Unlike Ti who is always pensive, Ni is outgoing and confident. I was really hoping that Ni's personality would somehow rub off on Ti to give him a leg up in the world, but it didn't work out.

Má also moved to Saigon with Ti because she couldn't live without him. Having both Ti and Má in the same little house was too disruptive for my brother's family and conflicts followed. Má took Ti back to the farm and she died a few years later. Ti mourned her like a son.

Phương became concerned about her son's mental state. He kept away from people and spent too much time in silence. When I returned for the funeral a few days later, she cornered me alone on a dirt road near the church cemetery and asked me to take Ti to America.

"Please give him the chance you had, when you were his age," she pleaded.

Not knowing if it was even possible, I said I would try. The year after, she died abruptly of a mysterious illness.

Her ghost still haunted me. The farm had not been the same without her. I missed her buoyant smile, her cheery sing-song voice, and her attention to detail. The spartan farm house was always clean and the yard swept with her there. She always had a roll of toilet paper, a fresh towel and soap for me whenever I came to stay. I never had to ask for anything because she had already taken care of it, including daily laundry drying on the lines.

• • •

In the morning, I got up early to take the walk that I had always looked forward to. It's my personal Camino, the one-mile pilgrimage from Hòa's farm down the main road to the village church and then to the cemetery, where Ba, Má, and Phương were buried. I know every step of this trail, having taken it every time I came back to the farm. This time, Hòa, Hương, and Xiu came along. We walked in the morning sunrise between farms and fields towards the cemetery near the coconut grove where Ti now lived.

Ba's concrete and granite tomb was still among the new ones on the men's side across from the women's. An open-air amphitheater church in between the two sides kept Ba and Má separated. Hòa gave me a bundle of lit incense sticks to pray for him. Then I prayed for Má and Phương. With the leftovers, I spread them around to the neighbors who didn't seem to have any recent visitors.

On the way back, I stopped by Ti's farm as the rest of the entourage walked on back. They wanted me to have time alone with him.

I found Ti alone in his hut as if he anticipated my arrival. We hugged and he invited me to sit down on a plastic chair on the concrete floor while he went out to fetch a fresh coconut. With the machete, he hacked off one end of the green drupe and stuck a plastic straw in for me to sip. This is something he had always done for me every time I visited, even when he was still a young kid. I would have chopped off my own fingers had I done it myself.

I have been known to be a man of very few words, but Ti had me beat. He had a dramatic sense of saying nothing and expressed his feelings with his eyes like a method actor in a Japanese samurai movie. I was looking at a sad forty-year-old man who was about to cry, without uttering a word. Then he struck the match and lit me a cigarette. I obliged.

The two of us just sat there, blowing smoke to the tin roof without talking. A cigarette only lasted five minutes so I finally asked how he was doing, healthwise.

"I don't know, Uncle Hao. I have had a fever in the last few days. My back hurts a lot and I can't go out in the field. Thao is out there supervising the troops."

"Be careful with the back. You shouldn't be lifting heavy loads." It was useless to advise him.

I stood up and looked around the hut. It was cluttered with cooking pots and pans, electric fans, clothes hanging on lines, hammocks, and a few farm dogs. No decorations except for B&W photographs on the wall of Hòa and Phương when they got married, when they were young with Ti and baby Xiu. A small altar with pictures of Má and Phương took up a corner. Má was frowning and Phương smiling, the way I remember them.

"Let me call Thao. She would love to see you." Ti picked up his iPhone and made the call.

Thao came back in a few minutes. She blew in like a tornado of fresh air and cheered up the place.

"Hello Bac Hao. You look good!" Big smile. She was like Phương in many ways, but a lot more direct and much louder.

"Have you been to the cemetery? Did you see the new tomb for Ba?"

I said I did. In fact, it was the first time I saw it because Ba died just before COVID hit and I didn't come home for the funeral. With Thao around, Ti opened up and started to talk.

He explained, "I am sorry for you to see our family like this. We decided to live separately from our father because we are not welcome there."

"It's not that we don't want our dad to have a new life. He had been single for so long so we were happy when he decided to get remarried. But we haven't gotten along since." Thao sounded like an opera singer, telling a classic tale.

"She is young, a little older than us, but that's not the problem. It's something she said that made Ti mad," Thao added.

"What did she say?" I wondered.

"She said we don't love our father, that we are greedy and want everything for ourselves, the farm, the inheritance."

Now I began to understand the rift. It was none of my business, so I switched the subject to something less heavy.

"How is the mango and coconut business?"

"Anh Ti works so hard. Do you know that we haven't had a vacation forever? The last time I could drag him to Vung Tau was ten years ago, and I had to make him go with the excuse to take Ba to the beach. The boys enjoyed that very much." She had tears in her eyes.

A truck came into the driveway and Thao went out to greet them. They came from Saigon to pick coconut. Thao counted as they loaded the heavy drupes on the truck flat bed.

"They cheated us by two dozen, but I let it go," Thao rubbed her hands together. "It's OK to let them have some profit. We did fine without picking the fruits ourselves."

"You look very healthy, Uncle Hao. I hope I will see you again many more times," Ti opened up a little more.

"I am almost seventy now. You never know when it will be my last trip."

"I don't mean you. I mean me. I may go before you will," his eyes turned a little red. "I was born with a congenital disease, more like a curse. One of my kidneys was constricted. The surgery was not successful. They opened and closed me up without doing anything. It's a hanging sentence, I just don't know when."

I don't really trust the doctors in Vietnam with diagnosis and treatments. Ti's situation made me think of the mystery around Phương's death. She was a healthy forty-something and suddenly became forgetful, bloated, and she died within a year of an unknown disease. The doctors suggested that she had blood poisoning and could have been saved had they given her transfusions in time. Others suspected that the chemicals used to weed, feed, and spray the mango farms had caused her death. We would never know for sure.

"I am keeping very busy. The trees need tending to, all year round. There is no time to rest between spraying and harvesting," Ti mumbled.

Outside, under the trees, the tractor and all the spraying equipment littered the ground, along with bags of weed killers, fertilizers, and insecticides. Not much had changed with the business of growing mango.

It was high noon and I was sweating in the hut, despite the running electric fans. My driver came to pick me up to take me back to Hòa's place just before I melted. He walked around the farm and used his phone to record the rows of mango and coconut trees.

"This is big business, big money. Plenty of money," he chuckled.

•••

In the evening, after dinner, Hòa and I sat and talked under the mango tree.

"Life is very complicated here. You can't believe what I have to do with the inheritance issue." Hòa broached this subject knowing it had been on my mind.

"Why is that? In my case, the U.S. law is pretty simple. If I die first, my wife makes all the decisions with the money. If she dies first, I will decide. If we both die, the trust will divide all our assets to the ten nieces and nephews. We have already made our will and trust."

"Not here. You can't believe that I still deal with Phương's family demands," he lit a cigarette. "Here, even after Phương has died, her family still can get a share of our farm. I have to ask every one of them for permission every time I do anything. Last time I sold the old tractor, it was so complicated that I just gave it away." He flicked the cigarette ash in the direction of the dogs.

"Holy shit! Is that really the law here?" I figured the more complex, the more you pay government officials to resolve issues.

"Yes. I have total rights to decide on my half of the assets to give to Ti and Xiu when I die. But now I have a new wife, the equation has even more variables."

I have always known Hòa as a wise man who can solve any problem. He built a successful farm in the new-economic zone of Tay Ninh where nobody believed it could be done. He is a rich man now and can navigate any situation no matter what. I am sure he can figure this mess out, given time.

"Meanwhile, Ti is mad at me. He doesn't know what I have to deal with." He poured me some tea.

"Maybe he will understand in time." That's all I could say.

"I think he also suffers from chronic depression. I can't help him and nobody can. I think being with Má for so many years has done it to him. Her mental problems must have rubbed off on him."

I have seen that happen. In the last years of her life, she had vented her sadness and anger on everyone around her. It was unbearable for me to be with her even for a few days, listening to the same laments and watching her go about her days with angry eyes. Ti had spent his teenage years with her, day in and day out.

"It got worse when Phương died. The two women whom he depended on the most for emotional support had left him. He stopped talking and worked himself to death. I am really worried about him but I don't know what I can do for him. He was born a farmer and will die a farmer. There is no other path for him."

Hòa hardly ever drinks, but that night he bought a few beers to share with me.

"At our age, who knows who will go first. We all have different fates cut out for us, but I am glad we are all still alive." I was talking about the seven brothers.

"I am a farmer. This is all I know. Ti is a farmer so he will live and die here. His sons will probably be carrying on the same destiny. All I can do is to ensure the farm stays within this family so they can still have a decent life. Perhaps one day, one of them can break out of this cycle and go to college, become an engineer or something, maybe to go overseas and travel the world, like you." He clinked the beer with me.

The die had been cast. It was cast fifty years ago when Giải Phóng happened and I could not return. It was cast when Má and my brothers came here to this new-economic zone. It was cast when Hòa built this farm and now it is his world. Like the mango tree, Ti was planted in this soil and there he stays until the day he dies.

I received the cigarette Hòa lit for me. It tasted hot and bitter.

Two Wild Ducks

"Do you want to stay at my home tonight?" My niece Thi looked at me with her big brown eyes.

I hesitated. "I don't know. I have a hotel room. I have all my stuff there."

"We have a big house," She insisted. "Vy wants to see you too. We will give you a room with air-conditioning and a toothbrush."

"OK," I said. "But I have run out of clean clothes. Should I go back to the hotel first?"

"We have everything you need." She pulled out her iPhone and called her Mom. "Ma! Uncle Hao will spend the night with us. Bye!" Then she hung up. Just like that.

After the three-hour drive from the farm, I got out of the car with an aching body. The road was rough and the seat hard. We unloaded a few boxes of mangoes and a bunch of coconuts at my younger brother Hương's place.

Van, Hương's wife, had already cooked a pot of Phở for us. It's the Chinese hospitality that I love about her. She fed me a steaming bowl of noodle soup with raw beef slices while she sat around munching on coconut candies.

Vy, Thi's younger sister, came out from her room in a nice purple dress and was about to go out. A polite young man came to pick her up. He bowed to us and said nothing.

"She has a date," Thi informed me, matter-of-factly.

Vy yelled back as she left the house, "I will be back in two hours, Uncle Hao." She waved to me before climbing on the back of the motorbike with her friend.

"His name is Zung, also a very good student," Van said in her Chinese accent. "He was half an hour late and he didn't even say sorry. Vy will give him hell."

"She has a skin problem," Thi made sure I noticed the pimples they both displayed but her younger sister Vy had a real red face with many ripe ones. "It's in the genes. All the girls in our family have it."

"The two girls complain about their skin problems all the time," Van waved her hand like brushing off flies. "They said I should have chosen a better husband. They said I chose badly: skin problems, ugly, short, and poor."

Thi and Vy were at the late-teen age when acne was at its worst. They wore thick glasses and were very conscious of their heights since they took after my brother who was five foot two. Of all the seven brothers, he was the youngest and also the most undernourished.

Thi gave me a toothbrush and invited me to watch Korean movies in her room, lined with posters of movie stars on the walls and books in English on the shelves. The movie was great but the Vietnamese subtitles sucked. Meanwhile, my eyes watered and I sneezed like a madman.

"It's allergies," I said, pointing at the cats.

She apologized, "I am sorry, Uncle Hao. I am allergic too, but I have medication."

Vy came back during the movie and gave me a bottle of beer she had just bought, "This is a craft beer made by a couple of Spanish guys. The microbrewery is 'Lazy Duck' and the 'Tết' label is for this special occasion." She was savvy and trendy with what's new in Saigon.

They fought over whose room I would spend the night in. Since I was allergic to cats and Thi had two, I was to sleep in Vy's room and the two girls would share Thi's.

Before they said good night, Thi told me the plans for the next day:

"We will leave at 8:00 am and eat Dim Sum for breakfast. Then we will go to the book shop in the same Garden Mall. Then we come home for lunch."

● ● ●

Promptly at 8:00, they were up and ready to go. Dressed like two schoolgirls with backpacks on a field trip, they led me out to the main street and called for a Grab taxi. To compete with Uber, Grab fares were very cheap, so cheap I felt bad for the driver.

"From here to there is only a dollar. How can they make a living?" I asked Thi.

"The company pays them the rest. It's a promotion."

"Let's give them some more," I said.

"Okay."

The Dim Sum place was popular, with a ten-minute wait, and it was worth it. The food was typical Hong Kong and service was good, all for less than 20 dollars. The dumplings were smaller than in America but the ground pork was fattier, just the way I remembered. We fought for the bill and I won the privilege to pay.

"My dad does not want me to take money from any uncle," Thi had told me a long time ago so I could only give her money in red envelopes for Tết as I have always done with other nieces and nephews. This outing was my chance to treat them to a nice day.

At a small café upstairs of the mall, they ordered for me a strong cup of coffee with condensed milk, without ice. Since coffee would make their skin problems worse, they had fresh orange juice and then off we went to the huge bookstore that had everything from soup to nuts.

Vy spotted a nice ukulele hanging on the wall and fixed her eyes on it.

I asked her, "Do you play?"

"Yes, I want to but my dad said it would make too much noise. I only play my friends' instruments at school," she was about to walk away.

I took it off the wall and gave it to her. She strummed a few notes, "This one has a pretty sound."

"Let me get it for you. It sure sounds good," I went to the counter and paid. "If your dad says anything about the noise, you can blame me."

I asked Thi what she wanted as she was looking at the book-shelves. Nothing interested her because all the books were trans-lated to Vietnamese. I bought her a colorful satchel made of Thai silk for her to carry books. She loved to read and asked me to bring her books in English whenever I came to visit. For myself, I found a couple of instruction books on how to play the bamboo flute, complete with CDs.

After the perfect outing, we went back to the house. Thi had already asked her mom to make us Chinese tossed noodles and roast chicken. Even after a big breakfast, I was hungry again at the sight and smell of her homemade cooking.

Van said while serving us large plates of noodles, "All I want is for the two wild ducks to study. They are very good students and love to hang around us. In Vietnam, people believe that boys are yours to keep and girls will belong to other families when they get married. These two wild ducks will fly away and I want their wings to be strong."

Thi reminds me so much of my old self: studious, diligent, and focused, but not street smart. Vy has all that plus social skills. She is more feminine and artistic. I predicted that Thi would become an academic while Vy would be a businesswoman.

The girls bantered back and forth. Their competition with each other entertained me.

Thi took credit first, "The Dim Sum this morning was outstanding."

"Because I knew what to order," Vy fought for her share.

"No, I picked the place," Thi put the finishing touch on it.

"Look at Thi's eyes," my brother tapped me on the shoulder. "They look exactly like yours."

"Mine are red," I was still catching up with jet lag.

"No, the heavy eyelids, the almond shape, and the eyebrows. And the way you fix your eyes when you listen. You two are related."

I looked again. Thi had a mix of her Chinese mother's thick black hair and my brother's height, and in a certain light her eyes reminded me of my mother.

● ● ●

Hương was born just before my family moved from Da Nang to Saigon and before Má got seriously ill. Because of her failing health, an auntie raised him for five years before he was returned to Má, who by then did not have much energy or love left to give. He was only ten years old when I left Vietnam for Australia and I didn't see him until my return twenty years later.

After Giải Phóng, he grew up in the new-economic zone with Má when my family was banished there. He helped clear the jungle and grow cassava for a few years and when he turned 18, he went back to Saigon to venture out on his own. He got a coolie job in a sawmill with a Chinese family and then married Van, their daughter.

When I returned to Vietnam for the first time, Thi was only six months old. With very little hair on her head, she looked just like me. Hương and his new family were living in a tiny rented apartment about nine feet across and twenty feet deep. Downstairs in his shop facing the noisy street, he ran a punching machine that cut teeth into long steel blades. Coils of new steel stacked high waiting to be made into band saws. Acetylene tanks lined the wall. Above the workshop, Thi slept among the din of the traffic mixed with the rhythmic crunching of steel and the rising smoke from the welding torch.

Over time, Hương's business went well. Being one of the few services in town for the sawmills, he had a constant flow of customers who came to pick up new band saws and drop off used ones with dull and broken teeth. Hương hardly had any time to rest all day as I watched him sit at the machine in his shorts, naked from the waist up. When I could get Hương to talk, although rarely, he told me that I was lucky to be loved. For him, he never felt that from Má, although she had told him before she died that she wished she could have. She tried to finish knitting a sweater for Van but never finished.

"She always looked at me with angry eyes, like I reminded her of something horrible. I don't remember being held by her, even once." Hương looked away at the door.

Van added, "I wish Má could get to know the two wild ducks. They are part Chinese, just like her."

Hương choked up, "When Má was dying, Thi wrote Má many get-well cards. Má kept them under her pillow, along with letters from you."

"We are paying a lot of money for their education, and private classes. How is their English?" Van asked me for my assessment.

"Excellent! Better than most. Better than me when I was their age, before I went to Australia. It's amazing that they got that good without having been overseas."

"All their teachers are either British or American. That's why the classes are very expensive, but as long as I can make money, they can have the best."

"He really loves these two wild ducks," Van did most of the talking for Hương. "He never hits or scolds them even once. He says that these two girls were born poor and he wants to give them the best he can. That's why he works so hard."

Hương added, "Thi is going to the University of Saigon with a major in English. Vy trails a bit behind and the two always compare their grades to see who is the best."

● ● ●

Before I left to go back to America, Thi and Vy came to the Victory Hotel to have a farewell dinner with me. They dressed up. Thi wore a black silk blouse, Vy a black dress.

"I have a bad foot," I warned them. "I can't walk far and I will limp, slowly."

While traveling with friends through the Mekong Delta, my left foot began to hurt with all the symptoms of gout. It was one of the random attacks due to something I ate, beef and seafood in particular. This time, I blamed it on the Tết beer that Vy gave me. It was very yeasty and unfiltered.

With sandals on, I limped slowly. The two girls walked with me, offering me their arms, one on each side.

We found the restaurant in an alley off Pasteur Boulevard, a low-end place that served mediocre food for an affordable price. Service was poor. They gave me white wine even when I asked for red. They served Thi a very tough burned steak and she ordered medium rare. Regardless, the girls didn't complain at all as they enjoyed spending their evening with me.

For desserts, Thi and Vy liked their yogurt made from condensed milk. I had a piece of chocolate opera cake and a cup of tea.

"I am going back to school tomorrow," Vy lamented. "It is going to be so boring."

Thi whined, "And I will work, work, work."

"I am still working but I am eligible to retire any time," I said.

Vy's eyes lit up, "Please retire and come back here more often."

"Uncle Hao, I have one more question for you." Thi looked in my eyes the way Má used to do.

"What? Go for it."

"Why do you love us?" She leaned on my shoulder.

"You know why. Do you remember when I returned and you were still a little kid. You asked me why I don't live here, why I had to leave again. You were too young to know why, but you looked so sad."

Vy said, "I know why now, but I am still sad."

Thi changed the subject, "I wish our dad would enjoy life a little. He never went anywhere for vacation. He always works and works. Mom says he is as dry as tiles. We took him to Danang to visit his birthplace. He said he didn't know anything about the town because he was still a newborn when the family moved to Saigon, but I am glad we could take him away for a trip."

"I haven't gone back there either, since I was ten. We have no more relatives there anymore. Da Nang has become just another tourist attraction now."

"When are you coming back?" Vy got us back to the subject. "It has been too long since last time."

"I don't know but let's set a goal. Let's stay in touch and I will see you when I can."

They accepted that as an adequate answer, for now. They called for a Grab taxi and dropped me off at the Victory Hotel. Thirty minutes later, I got an email from Thi:

"Uncle Hao! Enjoy the rest of the trip and have a safe flight home. I will miss you until the day you visit Vietnam again."

• • •

Then I didn't see them for five years because of the pandemic. I retired from a long career with the federal government and was ready to enjoy more travels but I had to wait until I felt safe to get on a plane. I also heard that Thi had got married but I couldn't come back to attend her wedding. Finally, I got to spend a day with Hương and his family

As soon as they heard of my arrival, the two girls came right in after work. They had matured and looked much more lady-like despite the lingering skin problem. They had both lost their thick glasses after Lasik surgeries. Thi donned a gray business suit and Vy had purple hair and a few tattoos. Thi's voice was strong and certain, like a professor. Vy was a bit quiet and contemplative and her eyes spoke more than she verbalized.

"I have something for each of you," I said. I gave each of them a signed copy of my book *Skinny Woman in a Straw Hat.*

Thi held it close to her heart, "My uncle is an author!" She jumped up and down.

"I hope you like it. You will learn more about me and my generation."

Vy said, "Please write more. I want to know everything. Our parents never told us anything about themselves and the uncles. They wanted us to study and that's all."

Thi's iPhone rang the familiar ringtone and she picked it up. She walked away talking to a male voice and later came back.

"I have another job offer. They said they thought highly of me and offered me one hundred dollars more a month plus benefits. They pay for lunch, health insurance, and telephone costs. Now I have two jobs. No more sleeping in." She sighed.

She had already got a job teaching English. They loved her at the private school. With the new job, she would be developing curricula for English classes. They would pay her more than the teaching job and give her a career ladder. She was much in demand.

Thi made plans for us to meet at a Dim Sum restaurant for me to see all my brothers and their families. She ordered the usual classic dumplings, rice rolls, pea sprouts in garlic, plus a roast duck, the crispy skin served in Mushu wraps and the rest in a stir fry noodle.

Van was happy serving everyone. "I am a professional," she claimed the title as she scooped wonton soup into everyone's bowl.

"I am going to Hanoi with my husband tomorrow," Thi announced. She loves concerts and had bought tickets for a big show up north.

"I am going to Phuket Island," Vy competed for her airtime. She had a new gig as a marketing specialist for a tourism company. She is quiet and loves mountains. She has traveled to Taiwan recently and will go to Thailand next.

The meal was sumptuous, with the two girls by my sides. Afterwards, I fought for the check when it came and lost the privilege to pay. Reluctantly, I said goodnight to the girls as they had to go home and get ready for their trips.

● ● ●

Later at night, after the Dim Sum dinner and everyone had gone home, Hương and I had time to talk at his house. Hương announced he had actually stopped working. Turning sixty, his sinuses were totally shot and he couldn't smell anything. More than three decades of inhaling welding vapors in his saw blade business had killed every cell in his nose. His hands and knees got knobby from years of handling heavy and sharp objects, typical of people in the sheet metal trade. At his age, working with saws and power tools had become too tiring and dangerous. Besides, the timber industry in Vietnam was already dying after depleting all the remaining forests. All the wood came from illegal logging in Indonesia and Malaysia, and that soon would dry out too.

"Smuggled logs are all we cut now." Hương said, leaning back in the big ornate wooden chair in his living room. "I don't know the source where the trees come from, but one time, customs people found ivory in one of the cants."

I said, "You have done well, brother. It's amazing that you started with nothing and made a life for yourself: a nice home and a beautiful family. Congratulations on your retirement."

"Maybe I can pick up a hobby. I have none. I have no music or art talent at all. I don't even have friends."

"You are still young," I said. "Time to enjoy life a little. Look at the girls. They are so full of life."

Hương poured me a cup of tea, "They are the best things we have ever made. Vietnamese people prefer boys, but we don't have any. Instead, we have these two wild ducks, but look, they have turned out better than we expected. They make me forget about the misery our family went through, the starvation after the war, the hard work and the sacrifices my wife and I made for them. I am so lucky."

As always, Hương didn't talk much but he smiled a bit more. His smile was never full and free, but I was happy to see that he could finally sit back and enjoy what he built. They have launched into the world two brilliant girls who stand on their own feet and make their own decisions. The wild ducks did not fly away, instead they have paid them back with affection and joy. Beyond his small fortune, he had created his own happiness, something he had never received from Má.

Last Time in Hanoi

At the cremation service for my father-in-law, Nhe had asked me to take him to Vietnam. "This may be my last chance. My brother wanted so much to return to Hanoi just once before he died but he couldn't do it. I will go for both of us."

"Sure, Uncle Nhe, I will take you there. I will go with you," I promised.

A year later, Nhe and I bought tickets and applied for tourist visas for a few weeks' visit to Vietnam. Tâm, Nhe's daughter, and her boyfriend Jack also came along. Tâm is pure Americana with big hair and white teeth. As a marketing director for an IT company, she oozed confidence and assertiveness. She made sure we got good seats on the plane, free drinks and snacks when we waited in the lounge area. Jack was also a world traveler. They looked good together, young and adventurous.

"Daddy, did you bring your compression socks?" Tâm asked in her childlike, loud voice as we sat in a quiet corner of the San Francisco Airport.

"What?" He pointed at his ear. "I don't have my hearing aids on."

She repeated several times until he nodded.

"I can speak Vietnamese, but not much," Tâm laughed. She

spoke a few lines of Vietnamese without the proper intonations and the words came out funny. I wondered how she would communicate with her relatives in Hanoi.

Jack offered to carry Nhe's bag. He is a cool all-American kind of guy, calm and soft-spoken. I had no concern about Jack's first time in Vietnam. He is an Anglo so they would treat him like an outsider: with respect and indifference.

On the long flight, Nhe sat motionless in his middle seat staring at nothing for hours while everyone was asleep in the dark plane cabin. There must be a thousand things Nhe didn't say. What must go on in the mind of a son who had not seen his mother since he left as a young man and couldn't even return for her funeral? All his brothers are dead now. What would he find when he got there? Would he recognize the place? Would there be anyone there in Hanoi he still knew?

Nội Bài Airport was no longer the grimy and scary little place that I remembered from when I landed there twenty years back. Every day, big planes arrived from all over the world. Travelers lined up in air-conditioned passport and customs halls. No matter how many times I had been back, I was still in awe of the chaotic airport scene. Việt Kiều us were yelling over each other, pushing big carts loaded with boxes wrapped in duct tape, venting enough nervous energy to power a small city.

We finally broke free and got through the gate into the foggy air outside the airport. Shaking off the cobwebs in my head, I looked about for signs of Hà, my wife's cousin. He had emailed me earlier that he would wait outside the gate to guide us back to Hanoi, ten kilometers away. I had met Hà on my first trip to Hanoi twenty years back. We became fast friends after two weeks of traveling together. He invited me to his small apartment in the old quarter where he lived with his widowed mother. He cooked many meals and introduced me to all the family members on my wife's side.

Hà recognized me right away with my bald head. He hadn't changed at all over the last twenty years, still with smooth skin and small dainty hands and feet. Even in a winter coat, he couldn't have weighed more than one hundred and ten pounds. I introduced him to his uncle Nhe, cousin Tâm and her boyfriend Jack. Hà greeted them in English with a European accent, something he had picked up over many years living in France.

Twenty years ago, Hà had told me his plans, "I want to go overseas. I want to go to France to study. I want to show my mother Europe. I want to see the world." And he did. Hà found a sponsor to go to college in Belgium and became a lawyer. Just like me, he became a citizen of another country and only returned to Vietnam to see his mother.

"Thank you for bringing uncle Nhe home. He is the last and the oldest of the clan. Everyone is eager to meet him." Hà hugged me tightly.

"You look so much like my youngest brother," Nhe said. Nhe towered over Hà when they embraced. "When I left Hanoi, your father was only twenty years old. I am sorry about his leukemia. I am sorry I wasn't here."

Hà held Nhe's bony hand in both of his. "My father died young. He suffered for a long time. It was a painful death. Thank you for what you sent to help us. We knew that you did what you could. I will take you to see my father's grave tomorrow, and anywhere else you want to go. It will be my utmost pleasure."

● ● ●

"Welcome to the Hanoi Hilton," Tâm joked as she checked out their rooms, referencing the notorious and horrible Hỏa Lò prison known to American prisoners by that name. "The conditions here have much improved." The rooms were indeed like any standard American hotel I have stayed in.

Nhe, Tâm and Jack had made reservations at the Hilton. I chose to stay separately in a mini-hotel in the old quarter of Hanoi, much cheaper than the Hilton and closer to where Hà's mother lived. I wasn't keen on spending more than a hundred bucks a night to stay in a Hilton like every other standard hotel in America, but the main reason I chose the local hotel was my love for the street scenes in the old quarter that reminded me of the way Hanoi used to be.

The old quarter boasts thirty-six famous streets, each named for the particular wares they offered. My father-in-law and Nhe grew up in Hàng Gà, the Chicken Street, where Hà's mother still lived. Those who left Hanoi miss it like a long-lost lover. They write nostalgic songs about the lakes shrouded in fog and the small quiet streets lined with tropical almond trees and perfumed with the aroma of milk flowers.

It was a few days before Tết, the Vietnamese new year celebration. Hanoi's old quarter was bathed in a visual feast of bright colors. Red flags, red dresses, red flowers. Peach blossoms bloomed everywhere, in the streets, flower markets, hotel lobbies, and store fronts. It is a tradition in the North to have the red blossoms in every home. Rich or poor, one must have some.

After leaving Nhe and company at the Hilton, Hà and I walked through the old quarter. We found a famous *Phở* restaurant that had been around for years and went in. The storefront opened like a cave and the vapors from the boiling pots steamed up the sidewalk, inviting local customers in for a hearty bowl of hot rice noodle soup topped with thin slices of beef. The small pieces of red chili were killing us, but we both added several to the broth, along with mint and a squeeze of lime. It had been a long time since I last tasted Hanoi *Phở*. It was everything I came for, the purist kind of beef noodle soup and not the fusion varieties in Saigon. I grew up in South Vietnam and had only read about Hanoi in literature. If Saigon was the pearl of the Orient, Hanoi must be pure jade. It was the birthplace of fine poetry and romantic music. Even the way the people talk had more finesse, at least that's how we southerners felt.

Afterwards, Hà and I made our way to his mother's apartment in the old quarter. We passed many new restaurants and shops. "I have been gone for a while now, so I am exploring Hanoi too," Hà said in his Hanoi sing-song voice. "I have to be careful with what I eat or I will have stomach problems." His sweet voice sounded just like Diep, my wife.

● ● ●

That evening, I walked to the Hilton to meet Nhe, Tâm and Jack. Hà had to spend time helping his mother with chores and preparing for Tết. The four of us found a nice, quiet Italian Restaurant across the street from the Hilton.

"Daddy, tell me my history," Tâm asked, sipping a glass of red wine. "I was too small to know and you never told me the whole story. When did you leave Hanoi, Daddy? Why?"

"I didn't want to bother you with the past. You need to look forward and leave Vietnam behind."

Tâm insisted, "We are here now and I want to know. I am a grown woman and I can handle it."

"This is good, please keep talking," Jack pulled out his phone and started recording.

"It was 1954 when my brother and I decided to go South. That was the last time I was here in Hanoi, more than sixty years ago."

"What happened then, Daddy? Why did you have to leave?"

"The North had already turned communist and they had persecuted many intellectuals and potential dissidents. Almost a million people fled to the South in fear of the new regime. My brother and I were among those refugees. The other two brothers did not want to leave Hanoi and they remained with my parents. I thought I could return once things settled but they never did. North and South became enemies and fought for twenty years. And when it was over in 1975 with the fall of Saigon, we were refugees once more and this time to the United States."

"What about your parents, Daddy? Did you see them again?"

"They died during the war. First, your grandfather in 1968 and then your grandmother not long after. I could not return to attend their funerals. My two brothers didn't survive. Through relatives in France, I sent money to help them all those years, but it was impossible for me to come home. I just couldn't. I thought I never could even afterwards. I was a refugee from the North and then became a military doctor for the South. I saved many American lives in the war. To the new regime, I had committed a crime for collaborating with the enemy. I am glad nobody cares about that now that enough time has passed. The war has been over for 40 years and I can finally return."

"God! I can't imagine what that's like. What if I couldn't visit you, knowing that you were there, somewhere in the world. I would miss you so much."

"You were only three when we left Saigon. We lifted off the runway as they shelled the airport. We were lucky. Our family was evacuated first because I was a military doctor and had saved many American lives."

"What happened then, Daddy? How did we end up in Pennsylvania first, and then California?"

"We were airlifted to an aircraft carrier and they took us to Guam. Supposedly, we should have gone to Camp Pendleton in California but there were protests against Vietnamese refugees so they took us to Arkansas and from there we went to Pennsylvania. We lived in Pittsburgh for a few years and I worked on getting a license to practice medicine again."

Tâm wanted more details, "So, how come we left Pennsylvania, Daddy?"

"You were only five. There was a fire. We were on the second floor. I threw a mattress out the window and dropped everyone on it. I jumped last and broke my leg." He tapped his right knee.

Tâm said, "I remember the fire. It was so scary I must have put it out of my mind."

"What caused the fire?" I asked. "Did you ever find out how it started?"

"Arson. Someone didn't want us there. The fire started in the stairwell and so we had to evacuate through a window. I decided we were not welcome there in Pennsylvania. Time to go to California where more Vietnamese had settled."

I knew that he came to California to join his brother, my father-in-law, who had settled in San Francisco. But for the almost forty years I had known Nhe, he had never told me this story about the fire.

● ● ●

Every day, Tâm and Jack bought tickets for museums and nearby attractions to play tourist while I spent time with Nhe. Like many foreign visitors in Vietnam, they had a long checklist of places to see and restaurants to eat in. They were glad that I could keep Nhe company so he wouldn't slow them down.

Nhe and I both loved to walk around Hoàn Kiếm Lake. Almost everything about the city had changed over the last decades, but this small lake right in the middle of old Hanoi had not. Surrounded by enough green space to shelter it from the tall buildings and construction cranes, it still looked like the iconic postcards of old Hanoi. We sat on a bench in the morning fog talking about the history of Vietnam, embroidered in legends and myths. In many cultures, legends sometimes converge around mighty swords. It was told that a Vietnamese king received a sword from an old turtle emerging from this lake. He used that sword to defeat the Chinese invaders from the North and then returned the sword upon his glorious victory, thus the lake is named Hoàn Kiếm, "returned sword." In the middle of the lake, the small turtle pagoda still stood in honor of the king and his sword.

"I used to fish here when I was a kid," Nhe said. "The water was clean and the fish were good. Mom fried them to a crispy brown and covered them with fresh herbs. I wouldn't do it now. Look at the dead tilapia floating here." He sighed.

I asked Nhe if he still recognized much of Hanoi from his childhood.

"So much has changed. I don't recognize much. So many people now. Cars, motorcycles, noise. I used to walk around the lake or ride my bicycle in quiet. Even the way people talk, they don't sound the same as the old Hanoi. It used to be pure. So many people have moved in from the countryside. The language today is mixed with so many other accents."

Indeed, like the language, everything about Hanoi is no longer pure. The streets in the old quarter don't sell what they were famous for in the past. High-end restaurants, massage parlors, and shops selling trinkets to tourists have taken over most storefronts. Once you see one street, you have seen them all.

We heard from a distance the sound of a bamboo flute. An alluring and haunting song floated across the water and reached us. Nhe hummed along a few lines and wiped his eyes.

•••

Hà had made arrangements for us to visit the cemetery where Nhe's parents and his two brothers were buried. We traveled ten kilometers outside Hanoi to a village where Hà's mother came from. All the remains of the deceased in the clan were moved there so the living can visit them together. The village's Buddhist temple was in better repair than the last time I came here twenty years back. The cemetery was also well maintained and cleaned up for Tết. Flowers and burning incense sticks decorated almost every grave. A cow and her calf grazed the grass between the tombs. Only in cemeteries would one find such fine, free grass.

Hà's mother greeted us at the cemetery. She recognized me right away. This was her first time meeting Nhe since she wasn't married into the family when Nhe left Hanoi sixty years ago. She guided us to the plots where a row of headstones announced the names of Nhe's parents and brothers. Hà unpacked a roll of incense sticks for us to light and place among the paper money that we burned, sending smoke everywhere, across the field, up in the air, mixing with the fumes from other graves. The whole landscape of the country the days before Tết was blanketed in a pleasant and acrid smoke that I associate with holidays, cemeteries, weddings, and funerals. It is a language that the Vietnamese speak, without words, floating in the air.

He prayed for a long time. His hands shook as the ashes from the incense sticks grew long and dropped to the ground. I heard him mutter words, muffled by his uncontrollable shaking.

• • •

Nhe had asked Hà to make a list of all the relatives and invite them to a dinner on his behalf. He picked the most expensive place in Hanoi, the seafood buffet at the Nikko Hotel. Nhe made a big fuss about it, making sure to get a private room away from the crowd.

The relatives, 27 in all, arrived in the lobby where Nhe waited near the large bonsai peach tree covered with Happy-New-Year gold leaflets. Nhe bowed to the two widows of his deceased brothers. They held hands with tears streaming down their cheeks. "I am sorry for your loss," they said to one another. There was not much else to say, but all was understood.

The two families in Hanoi had grown exponentially, with children and grandchildren. Nhe had a list that Hà had made for him to help match faces with names.

At the head of the adult table, Nhe stood up to say a few words. He stood silently for a long time to compose himself. Finally, in a trembling voice, he thanked them for coming.

"My dearest relatives. I am sorry I took so long to come back. I left Hanoi in 1954 so it has been more than sixty years. Believe me, I didn't mean to go away that long. I am speaking for my brother who can't come back with me. He is with us in spirit now. I know he is. He asked me to do this for both of us. I am fulfilling this dream for both of us. This meal is for the family reunion. Please enjoy."

The Nikko did not disappoint. The buffet couldn't be more sumptuous. Lobsters, oysters, roast beef, all sorts of pastries and ice creams. The kids tried all the desserts. Tâm got acquainted with her cousins in a mishmash of half Vietnamese and half English. Jack looked lost but he had gotten used to his role as an outsider.

"I haven't had a chance to talk with you much. We have been so busy, both of us," Hà said to me after we sat down.

"True, why don't we go out tomorrow, just you and me. We can spend a day in leisure. Your job is done now. Thanks for helping Nhe with this reunion."

"Tomorrow, I will come by to get you. I have stories to tell you." This last part sounded like a warning.

● ● ●

Hà and I were alone the next day. We walked around the lake as Hà pointed out the milk flower trees I had heard about in romantic songs. "The French planted them back then to mask the smell of the public toilets. You can imagine the public bathrooms. Very strong."

My fantasy about the beauty of the milk flowers portrayed in romantic songs was shattered. Regardless, I was happy with this new-found knowledge about these iconic trees. We found a coffee shop overlooking Hoàn Kiếm lake and ordered some lotus green tea. I dipped my nose into the fragrant steam.

"This is no vacation for me," Hà got to the point. "I can't wait to go back to Europe."

"What's wrong?" I asked, even though I knew the answer.

"They always find faults with me. I can't do anything right. I prefer to hang out with you. You don't judge me."

"I am not judging anyone." I really meant it.

Hà's voice shook as he continued, "They blamed me for giving uncle Nhe bad advice. He asked me what he should put in the red envelopes for the kids. I said two-dollar bills because they are lucky money. They told me that the banks don't like to exchange small bills. I should have kept my mouth shut. Uncle asked for my advice and I should have said I don't know."

"I am sorry. You are an outsider now, just like me. Don't worry about it," I said, trying to comfort him.

"Then it got worse. Today they said I did something terrible. Uncle asked me for a list of names of all the relatives. I made a small mistake with the accent marks on the word. Instead of Thành, I just wrote down Thanh. They said only parents can change kids' names. How dare you do that?"

"That is so mean," I agreed.

"It is all because I am *bisexual*," Hà finally said. "I am forty years old and they keep asking me why I am not married, why I don't have kids, why this, why that. They should know why. If I am not happy, I can't make anyone happy."

"Here, they don't leave you alone. At least your mother understands. Right?"

"Even my mother. She hasn't let it go. In Europe, I am respected for who I am and what I do. Here in Hanoi, I don't belong." Hà's eyes were liquid like the lake.

● ● ●

On the eve of Tết, Hà and I were in the streets waiting for the fireworks. We threaded our way towards Hoàn Kiếm lake but couldn't make any progress. Young people on motorcycles parked all over the roads and even the sidewalks. We found ourselves next to the old Hõa Lò prison, the dreaded Hanoi Hilton. Hõa Lò literally means the furnace and it has a bloody history. The French built it to detain, torture, and kill thousands of Vietnamese resistance patriots. The North Vietnamese kept their own dissidents there to die and, later, American POWs, to use as bargaining chips for an American withdrawal.

The fireworks lit up the foggy sky and showered hot embers down on us. The smell of gunpowder permeated the humid air. We watched balls of fire explode above the city and felt the deafening booms echo against the concrete buildings. I thought of John McCain, the American hero. He was dropping bombs on these people before he was shot down. They fished him out of another lake not far from here and beat him up before they put him in the Hanoi Hilton for five years. More than forty years had passed and the young people born after the war had no memories of those days.

After the grand finale, the crowds moved like water draining from a broken dam. They went to pagodas and temples to burn incense and offer money to the gods. They prayed for loved ones. Then the pyres began. Residents burnt paper money and fake gold objects in front of their houses, some of the flames were six feet high. Street front altars offered plenty of beer, wine, rice cake, and boiled chickens. The dead may not need the burnt money, but that is all that the living can give. The gods may not eat the boiled chickens but maybe they will be kind to Hanoi people for another year. No war, no hunger.

Nhe and company had already gathered at Hà's mother's small apartment when we arrived after the fireworks. It's the second floor of the three-story house where Nhe grew up. The rest of the house had been sold to other people living above and below her. In the sparsely furnished living room, she still kept the old piano that had not been played for ages. An altar occupied a whole wall lined with pictures of Nhe's grandparents, parents, and brothers. Fruits and incense sticks completed the display. The balcony served as the kitchen with a couple of kerosene burners. She had prepared the traditional dishes for the midnight Tết dinner. I loved the pork hocks stewed with bamboo shoots. Nhe savored the pickles eaten with the sticky rice cake stuffed with mung beans. Tâm and Jack took pictures of the food and asked questions about every dish. Hà did his best to explain to them what the dishes were supposed to symbolize.

Nhe thanked Hà's mother for the feast, "It has been too long and I have forgotten all about Tết. This meal reminds me of the home I had lost long ago. I feel like I am back in Hanoi with all my parents and brothers, before heaven and earth changed places."

"Welcome back, dear brother," Hà's mother said, her hand on his shoulder. That's all that needed to be said.

● ● ●

The last night in Hanoi, Jack and Tâm looked for the most expensive restaurant in town, of the ones that were open. Choices of eateries were limited during the few days of Tết because the Vietnamese traditionally close down business for seven days. The Argentinian Steakhouse was one of few establishments open for Tết to cater to tourists. The place was packed with Australians and Americans.

"I hope it is worth the wait," Jack said, looking hungry.

"There is nothing else going on in the whole city. This place looks just like San Francisco. I don't see any locals, do you?" Tâm asked.

Indeed, it was high-end. Fifty bucks for a filet mignon. Twenty for a salad. Wine lists were complete with labels from Napa Valley and Bordeaux, France.

"It is my treat," Nhe said. "You have been good to me. Thank you for taking me home."

After a half hour wait, we got seated at a small table upstairs next to an open window. The space was tight but intimate. Outside streetlights cast an amber glow against the old Cathedral with the statue of Regina Pacis in front.

After we sat down, Tâm and Jack showed me videos of Hanoi street scenes from a rented Vespa, contents to be added to their Facebook posts. They planned to go back to Hanoi again and travel to all the towns in Vietnam. Lucky for them, they had much to explore and nothing to miss.

"Hao, I have a story for you, since you are a writer." Jack showed me pictures of naked dog carcasses on a storefront table. "It should be written from the perspective of a dog in Hanoi. One day, he escapes and gets adopted by an American couple."

I thought that was not bad. Maybe one day I might write that novel.

In a separate banquet room sat a clan of two dozen Vietnamese. They were loud and drunk. Bottles of red wine were passed around. "Dzô Dzô!" they yelled. The eldest in the dark suit made a speech and everyone clapped. The women compared their diamond rings and gold bracelets. Children fought over chunks of rare roast beef.

"We are so unlucky. How come we always end up with a noisy crowd?" Hà complained in his lovely voice.

"They must be the beautiful people of Hanoi," Jack said, cracking a sarcastic smile.

Tâm said, "I have seen really wealthy people here. Plenty of money. They drive BMWs, big SUVs, here in Hanoi. I even saw a gold convertible in the street. How do they make that kind of money?"

"Blood money," Hà's voice rose above the din. "Here, these people own everything. They own hotels, airports, the police, factories, and the whole country."

The steak and salad were up to the gourmet standards for Jack and Tâm. I sipped on a glass of fine Cabernet. It tasted bitter.

Nhe seemed very quiet. I asked him if he had found what he was looking for.

"At least there is no war, no famine now. People don't have to flee for their lives anymore. Too bad generations have been wasted, millions of lives lost, and hundreds of thousands like us became refugees in foreign lands. I am so glad I made this trip. I got to see my nephews and nieces. I paid respects and burned incense for my ancestors. I enjoyed Tết and remember all I had long forgotten: the red peach blossoms, the rice cakes and the smell of incense smoke. I have done what I promised my brother in Fremont. I am grateful."

I asked if he would like to come back to Hanoi again. After a long pause, he said, "This may be my last trip. I would rather remember the way it was. It's always more beautiful to think of the old Hanoi, my parents and brothers, and the music of my youth. It's what I was looking for."

Hà, Nhe, and I had come to look for *Đường Xưa Lối Cũ*. Like many Việt Kiều's, we tried to go back in time to look for the Old Village Road in that song, a dirt path shaded by bamboo hedges and moonlit at night. The sound of the bamboo flute still floats above the lake, luring the wanderer to return. He longs for a mother who no longer lives. He searches for the girl he loves, but she has married and moved to a world far away.

What I Wish I Had Said

The day my mother died, I went fishing. After getting a tourist visa and airplane tickets for Saigon, I had nothing better to do. I had to wait three days before I could get on the plane. It was a gorgeous April day in Virginia and Má would have liked me to enjoy it. I grabbed my fly rod and fishing vest and drove up Shenandoah Mountain.

The Hughes River water level had dropped a bit, despite recent rains. I hooked three trout, one large enough to break the tippet. I didn't land them, but that's not important. It was just nice to spend a beautiful afternoon with thoughts of Má in my mind.

When I said goodbye to her the summer before, she insisted on paying for dinner even though I was the rich Việt Kiều. She was already frail, very frail. She was full of grievances about Ba and how nobody wanted to hear her stories, which I had heard so many times before. When I took a taxi to the airport, she trailed along in a cyclo for a while. I looked back at her. It felt like the last time. It was.

Soon after I returned to the States, she stopped writing. I sent her money and a get-well card when I heard she was ill. She didn't respond. She must have decided to die. She must have thought she had outlived her usefulness. She didn't know that I didn't need her for her utility. I just wanted her to live.

Again, I landed in Saigon. This time, Má was not there to greet me. At night, the city looked less poor than it did in the daytime. A few streetlights cast a yellow glow against the jungle of houses, crowding together without any room for trees to grow. I couldn't see any garbage littering the streets in the dark. The following morning, I rented a car to drive to Tay Ninh, where Má had lived since Giải Phóng.

I arrived at the farm by noon. Incense sticks and white candles burned at her altar in the living room. Her picture gazed at me with sad eyes. I broke down crying like a wolf howling at the moon.

My brother Hòa and his wife Phương let me stay in Má's part of the house. Her house hadn't changed at all, the same griminess that was typical of the tropical climate clung to the walls, but without her voice and shadow moving about. It was so quiet without her. Phương showed me the stains on Má's bed, where she had spent her last days.

"Má was waiting for you to come back. She always asked for you," Phương told me. "She was so lonely. Her sons in Saigon didn't visit enough. The ones overseas were too far. The day before she died, she was getting ready to go to Saigon to see a doctor and spend time with her grandkids. She packed and packed, but that afternoon she didn't get up from her nap."

I slept on the tile floor in Má's house. It turned cold at night. Jet lag disturbed my sleep. I woke up every hour, stared at the ceiling and listened to the geckos make their ticking sounds. The sun came up at six as it always does and I followed the morning light toward the graveyard. I stopped by the village church to thank the priest. It had been too long since I went to church. Má was not much of a Catholic when she was alive, but it was a comfort to know that he held a memorial service for her the Sunday before I arrived.

I missed her funeral by a few days and she had already been buried. A fresh block of cement and a wooden cross marked her burial plot. She rested under the shade of a tall Eucalyptus tree beside my brother Hoa's mango farm.

Hòa was working the field as I walked over to him. He finished what he was doing, wiped dirt on his pants and said, "Brother Hao, I am sorry you couldn't be here in time, but now you can do the work to build the tomb for her. It's your job now."

Later when I met with the local contractors, I asked them to use the best tiles and granite and I planned to stay to see the tomb finished.

That night, Ba talked with me, father and son, something we rarely did. I asked him what killed Má. He said many things, including TB, chronic asthma, heart problems, and severe depression. She was an old tree with old roots that couldn't stand forever. She was malnourished, had lesions in her lungs, a collapsed spine, and side effects of so many medications that the local pharmacist sold her. Her heart couldn't take it anymore.

"She was getting treatment for TB, but the disease didn't kill her. It was her heart," Ba said.

Tuberculosis still killed my people. The new-economic zone was a breeding ground for the bacteria and the disease, further punishment for those sacrificed by Giải Phóng. The local people worked and drank themselves to death, generation after generation, without healthcare or education.

Early in the rainy season, the sun was baking the cracked earth, but the rains had not arrived yet. It's always hottest before the first drop of water is squeezed from the sky. A rolling blackout came. Without electricity to run the fans, we had to find relief however we could. It was torture in the windless hot air as I tried to nap in a hammock under the large mango tree next to the house. Even the locals complained about the heat. Ba drove Hòa and me and the grandkids to a canal to cool off. After about fifteen minutes in the weedy water, I found a leech sucking on my leg. Blood kept coming out after Hòa pulled it off.

●●●

Over dinner under the mango tree, Phương and Hòa were in a better mood. They had cared for Má a long time and her illness, both physical and mental, weighed heavily on them. Without her, a palpable sense of calm fell over the farm.

Electricity came and went every few hours, and blackouts usually coincided with dinner time. As we ate dinner by candle-light, the sky suddenly lit up in bright bursts of lightning followed by cracking thunder. Winds blew out the candles, but no rain fell from the angry sky. Little black bugs played with the candles' flames and fell into the rice pot. They littered the floor like black beans.

"Tomorrow, we will be picking mangoes. Are you going to work with us?" Hòa asked, slapping me on the shoulder.

"Yes! I can work," I called back to him, my enthusiasm getting the better of me. I'd soon see if an American bureaucrat could survive a day as a Vietnamese farmer.

Hòa rounded up five workers from the village to pick mangoes. We started from the farthest corner of the farm and worked back.

Picking mangoes on a windless, hot day was a living hell. I held a long bamboo pole, pulled off the greenish fruits fifteen feet above my head and added them to a basket. Keeping a twelve-foot bamboo pole steady and aiming its tip at a small target above your head is not easy. My upper body strength was tested, especially since I didn't do this for a living, 12 hours a day.

In the courtyard, Hòa divided the mangoes by type and size into three different piles. After a quick, late lunch of bananas and sweet potatoes, we went back to work. Everyone was sweating in the heat but continued picking. Even the kitchen lady came out to shuttle the full baskets back to the house.

A big truck arrived from Saigon to pick up the mangoes. The driver promptly hit the hammock to snooze and save energy for the long drive back. His two guys went to work helping with the packing and weighing. At least they were in the shade.

All the loading was completed by late that night. Dinner was served to all involved, but nobody could eat much after such a long, hard day. The meal was over pretty quickly before people went home to crash. The driver waved as he drove away with two tons of the best mangoes in the South.

"How are your arms?" Hòa asked as he rubbed my drooping shoulders.

"Like noodles," I humbly admitted.

"We do this a dozen times a year," Hòa said. "Today I had the most expensive worker in all of Vietnam. How much do you make in America?"

I thought about that for a minute before deciding not to reply. The farmers here made two bucks a day while they paid me more than ten times that for an hour sitting at my desk.

• • •

Over dinner that night, Hòa and Phương told me stories about the years when they first arrived at *Kinh Tế Mới*, the dreaded new-economic zone. While Ba was in a re-education camp up north, Má alone had to keep my young brothers alive in the jungle frontier.

"For the first five years, we were hungry day after day. There was no rice, no *Nước Mắm* even," Phương began in her sing-song voice. "Whenever we could dig up a basket of cassava, everyone gathered to eat together. I was a street vendor, selling porridge and cassava cakes and the family ate what I didn't sell. Anh Hòa worked at the brick factory across the street and he had to steal engine oil to trade for rice. Baby Ti, my son, was in a basket all day without anyone taking care of him. Sometimes, I had to wash the feces off his clothes and hair. Má sold the rest of her gold teeth to give money to Hoa's business rolling contraband cigarettes."

"Má used to buy and sell little things in the village market to make extra money. Every time you sent us a care package, she kept the vitamins and aspirins for us, sold the needles, buttons and thread. The women's underwear fetched a good price. One pair could pay for three good dinners so we could have meat and fish."

I loved her stories and her voice. If I could have captured them, kept them in bottles and made audiobooks of them, I would have.

"We have a special treat for you. Try this!" Phương served a plate of steaming cassava. They picked this cassava when it was a young tuber, about one inch in diameter. It was soft and sweet with ground coconut, salt, and crushed peanuts.

"We haven't had cassava for a while. We ate plenty of it back then, almost every day, and I had it up to my ears. Now it's pretty good," Hòa admitted, nodding approval.

"Talking about cassava, we made up a nickname for it," Phương said as she laughed out loud. "We called it boiled pig's feet because it looks translucent and pinkish."

That night, Phương served a kilo of jumbo shrimp that she bought in the market in town. "We finally have real shrimp now," she said, picking up a big one with her chopsticks and putting it on my plate. "We used to eat grasshoppers and called them shrimp with wings."

"There is one thing I can never eat again," Hoa said. "It's the frogs. Not the nice frog legs you fry in butter. The ones we caught were about the size of my little finger. We found them in the flooded bomb craters. You know how we caught them?"

"I have no idea," I said.

"You take a long bamboo stick and whip at them. Hit or miss, the shock stunned them unless you hit them on the head first. Then you scoop them from the surface. Má cooked them whole in a pot of rice porridge to give us some needed protein."

"So why don't you like them anymore?"

"One day, I was whip-fishing for them and fell in the crater. I fumbled around in the muddy water and my hand caught hold of something soft, like weeds. I raised and looked at it. It was human hair, a thick mat of black hair." Hòa shook his head in disgust.

Phương cut up a few ripe mangoes for me. The mangoes from the farm were the sweetest, especially the tree-ripened ones. Phương looked up at the sheltering arbor above us. "These are from this tree, the oldest and best one."

She showed me a few pieces of jewelry Má left behind: a wedding ring, a broken bracelet, and a watch with a rusty band. She told me to take the wedding ring home to my wife, but I told her to keep it.

"Of all the brothers, Má loved you the most," Phương said. "She used to say that you were the first one to leave her and you lived so far away. She kept every letter you sent under her pillow until there were too many." Her words brought tears to my eyes.

Phương continued, "A few days before she died, she said in her dreams she kept tripping because you had strung threads all over the house. I think she knew something."

Phương handed me a student notebook filled with Má's handwriting. "I want you to have this book, since you are the only one who will keep it. She was working on her memoir for a month before she died. She told her life story from an early age up to the time she gave birth to her last son. Then she stopped."

Má's hand was still strong in the first few pages, but near the end it was hard to read as her handwriting trailed and the ink became fainter. Her book read like a long goodbye. Much of what she wrote in those 20 pages, I had heard over and over—about the abuse she received from her mother and sisters in law. What was new were the details of our last day in Da Nang, when I was 10, before we moved to Saigon.

I had always thought that the reason my family boarded a military plane and moved to the big city was Ba's reassignment to a new post at the army headquarters. I also thought that he wanted to keep us safe by being in the capital city of South Vietnam, further away from the war. The real truth was we were running away from a sordid past and it may explain Má's poor health for as long as I can remember.

When Má was pregnant with my youngest brother, she couldn't do everything for us and relied on a housemaid to do all the chores. When she heard Ba's report that the maid stole our money and didn't feed me and my brothers, Má asked her questions but got no answers, only tears. Then Má sent her back to the farm where she came from. Not long after, rumors spread around town and Má didn't know why people were looking at her askance and with disdain. When she visited my grandfather, she got a scolding from her own father: "Huệ Anh! How can you be so cruel? How can you send a pregnant woman away? You must take responsibility for what happens in your household!"

Ba had lied to her and made her do the worst deed. For decades, she alone had borne the guilt and shame for casting a housemaid away, unaware that she was pregnant with my half brother or sister, someone I would never know.

That family secret had set our family on a downward spiral and may have explained her mental illness. At the end of her handwritten memoir, she ran out of words and died. Her heart failed her like Ba said. She died of a broken heart.

• • •

The next day, we went to the cemetery to inaugurate Má's new tomb. The tiled crypt was accompanied by a new slab of polished granite adorned with a picture of her gentle face framed with short gray hair. Below the picture, these words were engraved:

Teresa Đỗ Huệ Anh

1930-2001

Hòa planted a few lilies and two boxwood shrubs around her resting place. We burned incense and said our prayers. I cried until I found no tears left.

Má's tomb was just a small marker on this vast landscape. It was two square meters of earth, concrete, and rock, surrounded by others of the same. These graves were not for the dead who were already gone. They were for the living to remember and return to. They were the glue that kept families together, the role that Má played while she was alive. The role that she will play even in death.

I have always believed that the most important things need not be said. They should be obvious, felt and understood. I have explained to my friends that Vietnamese hardly ever say "I love you." They are words lovers utter in movies, rarely heard in real life.

Every time I went home to visit Ba and Má when they were alive, I set a goal to tell them that I love them but never did. It never seemed right. They would have looked at me funny like, "What's wrong with you? Have you become a real American? Have you forgotten that we already know?"

Every April, I set aside a few days to go fishing. Just me and the river. I listen to the whisper in the wind, the white noise of water rushing through boulders and riffles. They speak the words I don't.

Twenty years ago, I went back to say goodbye to Má, a few days late. She had already been buried. I supervised the local laborers to build a tomb for her. The night I accomplished my duty, it rained—the first real rainstorm of the season. First, I smelled the soil baking, its steam rising, then I heard the drops fall. A belting followed like whipping on the tin roof. Hard rain, the kind of rain from my childhood. Then thunder and lightning split the sky open with all the energy of heaven and earth. The wind howled. After half an hour went by, all was quiet again.

That's what I wish I had said.

Acknowledgements

I would like to thank many colleagues and friends for their helpful comments and feedback on various stories in this book. Special thanks are due to Jim Barnard, David Belden, Gary Turchin, and Claudette Sigg of the Berkeley Prose Group. The same goes to the writing group led by Joy Reichart, who also is my coach and spiritual sister.

In addition, thanks are due to Eli Elbogen for many edits and helpful comments on an earlier draft.

Thank you, Nina Sacco, for professional editing and help with promoting my work.

I am grateful to Sharon Coleman who helped me find the poetic voice and open the faucet for stories to flow.

I truly appreciate J.K. Fowler of Nomadic Press for recognizing the value of *Skinny Woman in a Straw Hat* and selecting the story "Red Mud" from this book for the San Francisco Foundation Literary Award 2025.

As a writer of creative nonfiction, I create characters based on family members and friends with intention to honor and remember them. I truly thank them for being parts of my life journey.

It has been a pleasure to work with Nick Walker and Azzia Walker of Autonomous Press to publish my first book, *Skinny Woman in a Straw Hat*, and now this second collection of stories in *The Old Village Road*.

Of course, I couldn't have finished this project without the loving support by Diep, my wife of 50 years.

Finally, the inspiration for my writing comes from my love for Vietnam, her people and the land, and most of all, my late mother.